C000299215

Legally Avoid Property Tax

To Malcolm

Enjoy the Savings

Best Wish

Ian

Legally Avoid Property Tax

51 Top Tips to Save Property Taxes and Increase your Wealth

Iain Wallis

Copyright © 2013 Ian Wallis

The moral right of the author has been asserted.

Apart from any fair dealing for the purposes of research or private study,
or criticism or review, as permitted under the Copyright, Designs and Patents
Act 1988, this publication may only be reproduced, stored or transmitted, in
any form or by any means, with the prior permission in writing of the
publishers, or in the case of reprographic reproduction in accordance with
the terms of licences issued by the Copyright Licensing Agency. Enquiries
concerning reproduction outside those terms should be sent to the publishers.

Matador
9 Priory Business Park
Kibworth Beauchamp
Leicestershire LE8 0RX, UK
Tel: (+44) 116 279 2299
Fax: (+44) 116 279 2277
Email: books@troubador.co.uk
Web: www.troubador.co.uk/matador

ISBN 978-1783062-911

British Library Cataloguing in Publication Data.
A catalogue record for this book is available from the British Library.

Typeset in Calibri by Troubador Publishing Ltd
Printed and bound in the UK by TJ International, Padstow, Cornwall

Matador is an imprint of Troubador Publishing Ltd

Disclaimer

This is a book aimed at providing tax tips for those of you who like me choose to invest in property and is intended for general guidance only.

It does not constitute accountancy, tax, financial or other professional advice.

The author makes no representations or warranties with regard to the accuracy or completeness of this book and cannot accept any responsibility for any liability, loss or risk, personal or otherwise which may arise, directly or indirectly, from reliance on information contained in this book.

Where possible, hyperlinks have been included to current rates and allowances.

This book completed in July 2013 reflects current UK tax legislation the current law and practices of the government and HMRC though these are constantly changing and may have changed when you read this book.

Please note that your personal circumstances may vary from the generic information contained within this book and the examples given and thus may not be suitable for you or your family. It is therefore essential that for accountancy, tax, financial or other professional advice you seek professional advice specific to your circumstances.

This book deals solely with UK taxation which for tax purposes excludes the Isle of Man and The Channel Islands. Nor is this a book about the taxation in foreign countries.

Writing a book is quite a daunting task! For making sure that it's friendly on the eye and free of minsprits I'm very grateful to Jon Finegold at www.keyline-consultancy.co.uk.

www.iainwallis.com

About the Author

Iain had an early introduction to business life when his late father started his own manufacturing company. As a teenager it was a great introduction to the world of business and though he became increasingly interested in the business, his father had no desire for him to join it citing the mantra "Father, Son, Bankrupt", so on leaving university, he trained and qualified as a Chartered Accountant in 1984.

He started his own accountancy practice in 1992, developed it and eventually sold it in 2007.

Iain bought his first investment property in 2006 and has continued since then to acquire property for himself and other investors. After an adult gap year or two, too young to retire, Iain realised that there was a need to help the increasing band of seasoned property investors who were paying too much tax.

Building on his experience of over 30 year as a Chartered Accountant helping clients like the readers of this book, and with all his property investing knowledge, he has created a niche accountancy and tax practice that deals solely with high net worth individuals; it delivers sound taxation advice and legal tax strategies that avoid, and thus save, thousands of pounds in tax.

Iain is also a powerful and entertaining keynote speaker, and uses practical, day-to-day examples to explain away the complexities of taxation – and, in particular, property taxation. He prides himself on his down-to-earth manner – and the ability to make saving tax fun. Iain engages his audience with humour, whilst at the same time delivering tax strategies that can save thousands and, in some cases, millions of pounds.

Iain was a keynote speaker at the largest property event in the property calendar, The Property Super Conference 2013 at Wembley, London, where he shared the stage with some of the best-known property experts in the UK, as well as high-profile speakers such as Karren Brady and Frank Bruno. Iain's presentation *Legally Keep More of Your Property Income* was a sell-out – it must be the first time Wembley has rocked to tax!

It's not all about property though. Although not a native until 2008, he lives in the county of Northumberland: close to glorious beaches and the hills of the Cheviots. A lifelong – and sometimes long-suffering – supporter of all sport played by England, Iain, along with his wife Fenella, had the good fortune to be in Sydney in 2003 to see England win the Rugby World Cup.

> *This is the one.*
> *It's coming back to Jonny Wilkinson.*
> *He drops for World Cup Glory.*
>
> *He's done it, it's over.*
> *Wilkinson is England's hero yet again and there's no time for Australia to come back.*
>
> *England have just won the Rugby World Cup".*

The immortal words of BBC Commentator, Ian Robertson.

On the 22nd November 2003, Iain and Fenella saw that wonderful event in Sydney as, after a three-week rugby holiday, they watched England win the rugby World Cup. "It was one of the best and happiest days in our life together," recounts Iain.

On 5th December 2003, Fenella's sister Davina lost her brave battle against cancer, the saddest day in their lives. This was not supposed to happen. Davina had done well through all the treatments and, with her deep faith, was well on the way to recovery. Little did they all realise how savage the cancer was. It returned with a vengeance.
Talk about 14 days of contrasting emotions and, yes, a reality check.

She was the same age as Iain, just 46, and left three wonderful children, a husband and a close family. So, please: follow Iain, and enjoy life, live every day as if it could be your last and, like Iain, give whatever you can, whenever you can, to Cancer Research.

Please note that £3 of the purchase price of this book will be given to Cancer Research.

A note about the examples

Throughout this book where possible I have used worked examples to facilitate explanation of the tax tip. For the avoidance of doubt, unless specifically stated all persons used for examples are UK resident, ordinarily resident and domiciled for tax purposes.

Where rates and amounts will change I have included hyperlinks to the HMRC website to allow you to have up-to-date information. That said, tax law and interpretations of it can, and does, change overnight; you should bear this in mind when applying examples to your real-life situations.

Unless specifically indicated otherwise, all persons used in the examples in this book are entirely fictional created simply to facilitate the explanation of tax tips. Any similarities to actual persons, living or dead are entirely coincidental.

As you work your way through you will see a theme developing from the names used in examples and I trust that my knowledge and love for the British & Irish Lions has ensured an equal representation.

Contents

CHAPTER 1

Introduction

Imagine having to write a cheque to the Inland Revenue for £1.8 million. Can you feel the pain? Can you see how many noughts that is? Can you imagine the joy of the taxman?

Do you feel sick to know that that that tax revenue will go to pay the benefits of those who chose not to work in our society?

What could your children or grandchildren have done with that money?

Now imagine that, instead of writing a cheque for £1.8 million, you had written a cheque for £360,000 – making a saving of £1,440,000! How good does that feel?

What could you have done with all that extra money? How would that have helped your life? Would that have enabled you to secure the future for your children or even your grandchildren?

And the sad thing is that this actually happened to a UK taxpayer. She had been using a non-specialist property tax accountant who, each year, had happily prepared her returns and collected a fee without thinking about what might happen one day. She was diagnosed with an illness that left her with less than a year to live. Suddenly minds were concentrated and her daughter, after frantic checking on the Internet, found and approached me wanting to know if I could help with a massive Inheritance Tax problem.

The answer, of course, was yes. Steps were put in place, even with such a short lifespan, to help keep the money away from the taxman. Alas, the illness was worse than initially diagnosed and she died within two weeks of our initial meeting. So the Inland Revenue picked up a very nice cheque.

You don't want to be the next person to write out another large cheque to HMRC do you?

Inheritance Tax is just one of many taxes that can potentially take a significant chunk out of your hard-earned income and wealth from property. Whilst in this case a lot of the wealth had come from property inflation, it was wealth nonetheless; wealth that should be passed through the generations, not – in my humble opinion – passed across to the Treasury.

There are many other taxes that will impact on a property investor. In no particular order, and depending upon your personal circumstances which we will examine throughout this book, the main ones could be Income Tax, Corporation Tax, Capital Gains Tax and Stamp Duty Land Tax.

In addition National Insurance and VAT could raise their ugly heads, along with a myriad of other direct taxes that we are unable to avoid whatever we do: fuel tax and insurance tax to name but two. For the smokers amongst you there will be tobacco tax and the drinkers – yes, you've guessed it: there's a tax there as well.

So why write this book and just who is it for?

First out let me say that this is not a tax manual. I'm sure that you have no difficulty dropping off to sleep at night. Wherever you are in your property journey, this is a book for you.

You might be a property investor or a property trader (much more later) looking at ways to reduce your exposure to taxation.

You might have a portfolio of property that's been providing you with income for many years that you want to protect from Inheritance Tax.

You may be the proud owner of a house free of mortgage debt, which you want to pass down to your family – without the taxman taking a share.

This book contains at least fifty-one tax tips and things that you should be aware of to legally avoid tax – whether you do your own self-assessment returns or pass everything over to your accountant. I want to make absolutely sure that you've not left any money on the HMRC table.

I want to help those starting out in the property journey to get the structures right to – legally – pay the least amount of tax possible. I want to assist those whose property business is up and running and want to retain as much profit as possible. I want to ensure that anyone investing in property has the perfect exit strategy – and does not let HMRC take 40%.

Those of you who have been lucky enough to go on safari will know that the 'big five' are the lion, the leopard, the cheetah, the rhino and of course the elephant – naturally the ones to see and tick off in your Eye Spy book of animals. In the world of property taxation the big five are:

- Income Tax

- Capital Gains Tax

- Inheritance Tax

- Corporation Tax

- Stamp Duty Land Tax.

Here, we want to *avoid* the big five – not stumble across them and then see a large tax bill!

Believe me when I say that you will stumble across them; sometimes they combine to make your life very unpleasant. Yet, armed with the correct knowledge, they can be avoided.

I want you to be aware of the pain that taxation can cause you – because when you are aware of that pain you take action. But then you knew that anyway, didn't you?

Within the big five, all will bite with varying degrees of pain – though Inheritance Tax can do the most damage, as demonstrated above. But it is also the easiest one to avoid.

To *avoid* tax requires careful planning but, above all, it requires you to take action.

As a mentor of mine says **"to know and not to do is not to know"**!

So read through this in its entirety – or dip in where you want to if you have a specific query.

You will find stuff that you can apply, take action and above all legally avoid tax.

- Chapter two sees a healthy debate about tax and tax avoidance and the rights and wrongs.

- Chapter three will examine whether you are a property *investor* or *trader* – and what to look out for to come to the right outcome.

- Chapter four will look at the deduction of expenses that are common to both investor and trader: don't leave money on the HMRC table by not claiming what you are entitled to.

- Chapter five will drill down further into the allowable expenses for those who fall into the property investment category and look at ways to avoid tax.

- Chapter six will contrast the fortunes of those who trade in property and look at some great ways to avoid tax.

- Chapter seven will look at the first capital tax where property values have a bearing on tax liabilities and consider the many strategies that can be followed to avoid them.

- Chapter eight sees a round-up of all the other taxes that could potentially impact on your business.

- Chapter nine saves the best till last; it looks at the second of the taxes driven by property values: Inheritance Tax. Without doubt the most vicious tax, but also the easiest to avoid with suitable tax planning.

- Chapter ten looks at what could happen if it all goes wrong! Provided that you stay legal and avoid tax – and do not *evade* tax – then this chapter will be of little concern. It is in there just in case you do capsize, or you think that you can outsmart the taxman.

This is a book about property and the impact of taxation on your property wealth and your property income. That said, there are however a multitude of tax steps that you can take to legally avoid tax throughout your tax-paying life and if you'd like to have my free Taxability Checklist, containing over 65 top tax tips, then please visit:

www.iainwallis.com/contact-me

Above all, please enjoy: Moira Stuart and Adam Hart-Davies are not wrong when they say "tax doesn't have to be taxing"!

CHAPTER 2

Tax Avoidance or Tax Evasion

2.1 Introduction

Little did I realise, as I sang along to the Beatles all those years ago, the importance of the lyrics from a song on the Revolver album, released back in 1966 when I was just nine. The song was called "Taxman" and bemoans how in the sharing of wealth, there was one for the taxpayer and nineteen for the taxman, a reference to the egregious rates of tax at the time. The song laments the fact that whatever you do be it drive, walk, sit or even try to keep warm you will be taxed.

Ok; so this was penned in the days when high earners were paying an effective rate of tax of 95% brought in by Harold Wilson's Labour government. The song was no doubt fuelled by the anger of George Harrison keeping only £5 from every £100 he was earning but the sentiments are as appropriate now as they ever were.

Whilst you will not be paying tax at 95% you may have a marginal rate of tax of 45% – so anything that can be done to avoid losing 45% of what you've earned should still to be looked at!

Lord Clyde famously said, in the case of Ayrshire Pullman Motor Services v IRC 14 TC 754 (1929):

No man in this country is under the smallest obligation, moral or other, so to arrange his legal relations to his business or to his property as to enable the Inland Revenue to put the largest possible shovel into his stores. The Inland Revenue is not slow, and quite rightly, to take every advantage which is open to it under the taxing statutes for the purpose of depleting the taxpayer's pocket. And the taxpayer is, in like manner, entitled to be astute to prevent, so far as he honestly can, the depletion of his means by the Revenue.

2.2 Tax Avoidance

So let's nail this thing about tax avoidance right at the start.

Her Majesty's Revenue & Customs or, indeed, the Chancellor of the Exchequer may not like tax avoidance – but it is perfectly legal. Let me repeat that, because it is so important: *Tax avoidance is perfectly legal*.

It is well-established that you can manage your affairs to legitimately avoid tax. So what if the actions that you take mean that you gain and the taxman misses out. Do you really want to pay more tax? Are you serious?

Ignorance is not bliss in life and certainly not with tax! Not knowing how you can *legitimately* avoid tax, or being scared of the taxman, is restricting and damaging your personal wealth.

You have a responsibility to yourself, to your spouse or partner, your children and grandchildren to take charge of these matters to maximise your personal wealth.

Everything in this book is completely legal, safe to apply and should be being used by accountants up and down the land. If your accountant is not, then you genuinely have the wrong accountant.

In terms of risk, where 1 is looking both ways before you cross the road and then checking again, to 10 where you are smacking a wasps' nest, these are all in the 1-2 range. There are some very aggressive tax schemes out there, but they are not for this book.

Jimmy Carr, amongst others, found himself in hot water for following such an aggressive scheme. But wait. He has done nothing wrong. Controversial maybe, but all he's done is legally avoided tax.

Now some of us may not like that, and it is for his moral compass to decide if he is happy with his decisions – but he has taken that choice through advice from his accountant and professional advisors. His advisors would be failing in their professional duty if they did not present these opportunities to him.

So please, please bury – no, not bury, smash the belief that tax avoidance is illegal. Smash it into thousands of little pieces.

That said, every accountant is taught at a very early age: "Don't let the tax tail wag the dog!" An action taken may save a load of tax – but does that action really make commercial sense in your specific case? Is it really worth the effort, or the risk, or the expense? Don't spend a pound to save a penny! So please bear that in mind as you make your way through this book.

Aggressive schemes pursued by companies or highly paid entertainers may not sit with your moral compass – but it has never been, and never will be, illegal to manage your affairs to avoid tax.

Ah, you may say. That's all well and good, but everywhere I turn I'm told that tax avoidance is wrong. So why are we being brainwashed into believing that tax avoidance is a problem for everyone?

Her Majesty's Revenue & Customs, (from now, simply 'HMRC') and HM Treasury have a shared objective of minimising the tax gap. The tax gap is the difference between the tax collected and the tax which HMRC think ought to be collected. In addition, you might have spotted that UK Plc. is a little short of funds at the moment.

To quote from the HMRC website:

> *We want to provide our customers with a level playing field, while maintaining the UK's international competitiveness. Our strategy for delivering this objective is through encouraging everyone to pay tax at the right time and vigorously tackling those who deliberately avoid their responsibilities.*

It continues:

> *In the UK, the tax loss from avoidance is estimated to run into several billion pounds across both direct and indirect taxes...*

(Direct taxes are taxes that individuals or companies pay direct to HMRC, such as Income Tax, Corporation Tax or National Insurance, whereas indirect taxes are charged on goods and services, such as excise duty, insurance tax and VAT.)

> *This directly affects the delivery of public services and long-term economic growth. Avoidance distorts markets, is economically unproductive and breaks the link between economic productivity and reward.*

Helpfully it tells us that:

> *The vast majority of our customers do not participate in tax avoidance and will stand to benefit from HMRC's anti-avoidance strategy. HMRC is taking a proportionate, risk-based approach to avoidance, which is consistent with HMRC's commitment to supporting our customers.*

Isn't it just wonderful that we taxpayers are now seen as customers; maybe, one day, HMRC will discover the concept of customer service and deliver a great experience. As agents to taxpayers we get a dedicated line but have you as a 'customer' ever called them on the phone? If you do have to, be sure to arm yourself with a cup of coffee and prepare for a long wait. Less helpfully, they tell us that *"it is impossible to provide a comprehensive definition of avoidance"* and thus it is, therefore, impossible for them to give any guidance to us poor impoverished taxpayers as to how they plan to "level this playing field".

So relax.

Don't you worry about our international competitiveness! Concentrate instead on doing what you can do ensure that, where possible, you follow every tip in this book to legally – and without fear or remorse – avoid tax and thus reduce your tax bill.

2.3 General anti-abuse rules (GAAR)

Just to add to the mix from April 2013 the long-awaited and much-talked-about general anti-abuse rules came into force.

The first thing to say is that this is not, as widely feared, a green flag for HMRC to ride roughshod over anything it didn't like. Fortunately for us humble taxpayers nothing has really changed. It is more aimed at egregious tax planning and schemes for those with a far higher risk profile to tax planning and schemes that are not covered in this book.

The general message is that *avoiding* tax, by making the most of the tax rules, (which is what this book is all about) is OK! However, taking steps that are *artificial or abnormal*, or which are *solely to escape tax* will fall foul of GAAR. In those circumstances HMRC will claw back the tax saved and, as ever, help themselves to penalties.

The only issue now is that what *you* consider to be fair avoidance might be different from HMRC; rather unhelpfully, there is no system to ask HMRC in advance if your proposed action will be acceptable under GAAR, or will fall foul of the rules.

Helpfully for us property investors, it specifically gives examples of 'flipping' and giving assets to your children to avoid taxes; these are acceptable actions as to the making use of current tax law; having waded through the guide it's safe to say that GAAR should not impact on those making the most of the available rules.

Tax *evasion,* however, is completely different – so, as M, would say "Pay attention, 007!"

2.4 What is tax evasion?

Whilst legitimate tax avoidance is legal and to be encouraged at all times, evasion is not legal and certainly not to be encouraged.

Put simply, tax evasion happens when people deliberately don't pay the tax they should. Tax evasion is a crime and everyone loses out because of it. Naturally, HMRC is committed to tackling tax evasion.

Before all the doom and gloom, it is important to point out that the law does not require perfection. It requires that you take 'reasonable care' to get your tax right. We are now, and have been for a number of years, under self-assessment; it is for you to provide all the information and get your tax right.

If you make a genuine mistake and can demonstrate that you took 'reasonable care' no penalty will be due. Alas, there is no legal definition of 'reasonable care' so common sense will prevail and the facts of each case.

If you "forgot" that you sold a property and didn't declare a capital gain that's hardly reasonable care and most likely tax evasion!

If, in the absence of a lost bill, you over-estimated some capital improvement costs when completing your tax return which was found to be excessive then you are unlikely to unleash the Harbingers of Hell at HMRC.

The three things to consider are:

- Have you under-declared your tax liability?

- Have you over-claimed tax repayments?

- Have you failed to tell them that you are liable to pay tax?

At its worst, tax evasion could find you serving time at Her Majesty's pleasure; while you will be guaranteed three square meals and a bed for the night it doesn't look too good on the CV! There are the high-profile cases of Lester Piggott (who was jailed for three years for tax evasion and stripped of his OBE) but it also happens to ordinary people.

Last year, a plumber was jailed for 12 months for tax evasion, demonstrating that HMRC is deadly serious in its clampdown on the black economy. Melvyn Careswell from Epsom in Surrey set up a company, MPC Heating and Plumbing, but he never registered his earnings with HMRC. Investigators discovered that, over a five-year period, he evaded around £50,000 of income tax.

Flushed with success, Chris Martin, assistant director of criminal investigations at HMRC, said: "Careswell stole from UK taxpayers by failing to pay tax due on his earnings and now he must face the consequences of his actions in jail."

As you will see in this book there are more than enough *legitimate* ways to avoid tax. So please, please, do not go down the evasion route.

Evasion means worrying every time you get a phone call from an unusual number, worrying about that knock on the door at some unearthly hour, and constantly being on edge. Life's far too short for that.

So please avoid – but don't evade!

As that annoying little rodent says, "Simples!"

CHAPTER 3

Who and What are You?

3.1 Introduction

Many people who start out in the property business call themselves 'investors' – but are they property *investors* or are they property *traders*?

They can actually call themselves what they like; however, although you may believe yourself to be an investor it is the facts of the case – and how you carry out your business – that will determine whether the *taxman* (HMRC) sees you as an investor or a trader. So beware.

Just to make matters worse, there is always a muddying of the waters – those areas where it is not really clear cut on which side of the investment/trading fence you may be found.

3.2 Am I a property investor?

Typically, a property investor will hold properties as a long-term investment; they will be the assets of the investor's business and bought both to produce rental income and, over time, capital growth.

A few words about capital growth and property investment.

Everyone has a view on property; it sparks much heated debate and wildly contrasting views. Depending on which paper you read, or which websites you browse, one day we are going to hell in a handcart – but, the next day, property is the best thing since sliced bread.

Certainly, in the last few years, the UK property investment industry generated much negative press, with the housing dip, which nobody foresaw leaving many landlords financially exposed. Those hit the hardest fell into two groups:

- Those who believed the glossy brochures and fell for the property-marketing hype. They bought off-plan in areas that they didn't understand, in the expectation of capital growth and predicted rental income that never arrived.

- Those who took advantage of all the cheap money (some of you may remember NINJA mortgages: No Income No Job or Assets) and borrowed to buy houses, and borrowed again to fund a lifestyle. Their borrowings compared to their debt (gearing) got out of hand – but they didn't care, as house prices were booming. Their failure to allow for property market corrections has left them with large debts which they are unable to fund from rental income.

In addition to this, the impact of the economy on household income has put unbearable pressure on some family budgets; despite interest rates being at their lowest since records began, we have seen repossessions rise and a very static housing market. Faced with such doom and gloom your family, your friends down the pub – indeed anyone without property knowledge – would advise against investing in property.

But it's not all doom and gloom. As with any investment, property investing can be extremely rewarding and financially beneficial – if simple rules are followed and you keep on the path you set out to follow.

So why invest in property?

Property, just like investing in shares, investing in your own business – or just leaving money in a savings account – will be a strategic decision. Any investment strategy (short, medium or long-term) that you follow will be based very much on the goals that you have set yourself. Issues you should have considered include your need for:

- Income today

- Income in the future

- Capital growth

- Control of the investment

- Where you invest

- The price you will pay

- The rent you charge

- The price you sell at

- The type of mortgage you have

- Passing the investment down to your family.

These should form the backbone of *any* investment consideration.

Why not shares, bank savings or a pension?

Traditional investments, such as stocks and shares, have one clear advantage: they are relatively liquid assets – i.e. they can fairly readily be turned into cash, if you need it. So, if you make an investment in ABC Ltd and then decide you don't like that, or you need access to some of your funds, there is a ready market for those shares and you can sell.

However, few of us have the time or, indeed, knowledge to play the stock market so, after a risk-assessment profile from an independent financial advisor (IFA), we abdicate responsibility to a Fund Manager. You wouldn't abdicate from the responsibility of looking after your children – so why abdicate from looking after your finances?

"But I like my money in the bank. I get a statement each month and I know it's there." Yes, that's very true – but here's the thing: the best rate currently paid by a bank to tie up your cash in a five-year bond is around 2.75%. A simple deposit account will pay 1.75% or less.

Inflation is running at a conservative 3% – so, in actual fact, you are *losing money* on your cash. Is that a good investment?

The vast majority of individuals don't have their own share portfolios, but rely on their pensions to provide for them in the latter years of life.

We are constantly told that the State Pension is a thing of the past. The government is reforming the State Pension for future pensioners – the published proposals include an option for a flat rate State Pension of around £140 a week for a single person. So our futures are down to the pension contributions we make, whether personal or through our companies.

In the good old days a company pension would pay out on what's called a 'final salary', which was geared around your last few years of employment – which, typically, would be the best. Collect your gold watch and ride off into the sunset with a handsome salary in retirement. For companies, however, that is an uncontrollable cost; so, over the last few years, companies have consciously moved employees to 'Defined Contribution Schemes', reducing their liability. This is based on an ageing population and longer life expectancy.

Defined contribution pension schemes are great for the company – but not as good for the individual, where the amount you put in defines the 'annuity' that will be bought, and thus your annual income when you retire.

No one would deny that we have seen an adjustment in the housing market since it overheated in 2007. Give three identical sets of figures to three economists and you will get three different opinions, purely because their opinions are based on *assumptions*.

Depending on which economist you went, to they would have a differing view of the house market. But, and here's the thing, even if the economic pressures that we are currently under in the UK move this cycle out to a longer timeframe, if you have invested wisely you still benefit from passive income – which will of course boost your pension/ household income.

What is an asset?

Like me, many property investors have read and continue to reread a fantastic book by Robert Kiyosaki. In *Rich Dad, Poor Dad* he talks about the difference between an asset and a liability. Quite simply an asset puts money into your pocket every month, while a liability takes money out of your pocket.

On this basis it is clear that our own homes are liabilities (unless mortgage or rent-free) as we need to pay the mortgage, keep them repaired etc. A properly sourced buy-to-let property, which produces positive cash-flow, is an asset: you receive money (rent) every month.

Look around your family and ask yourself if you have been buying assets or liabilities? Does the 52" super-surround cinema system with super sub-woofers that deafens the neighbours, put money in your pocket? Is the expensive (or even the cheap!) car on the drive an asset - or a liability? So do you want to continue buying assets or liabilities?

So why invest in buy-to-let property?

Why on earth would you want to invest in property? It's far too risky, surely.

The UK has a tradition of home ownership. The *2002 General Household Survey: a summary of changes over time between 1971 and 2002* shows that home ownership increased from 49% to 69%. However, there has been, and will always be, the need for rental property: economic factors, lifestyle, the moveable jobs market...

The Office for National Statistics (ONS) shows that the current UK population of 61.4 million will rise to 71.6 million by 2033. Mark Twain said, "Buy land, they're not making it anymore" and guess what: the UK is an island, so this population increase will put massive pressure on housing stock. Shortage of supply, coupled with increased demand, will impact on rental values. With a shortage in housing stock predicted to be at 750,000 homes by 2025, the demand for the houses which are available will be high.

Factor in that the average age for a first-time buyer who is not given financial help is now 37; so there will always be the demand for rental accommodation.

I well remember being on a property seminar and the presenter asking, "Who knows what 'yield' is?" He followed that up with "Who cares?" He is probably one of the many who stripped out all his cash and – then found that the rents were not able to finance the mortgages. Hopefully I've picked up some of his stock at auction once they were repossessed.

Luckily, the accountant in me did know and did care – but for him it was about the fantastic capital growth you could achieve at that time. The investing model, if it could be called one, was simply to buy the property, remortgage the property (sometime on the same day) spend the capital released and sit back and watch house inflation make you money.

The smart ones amongst you may have spotted that the rules have now changed significantly; the trick is now to buy below market value and secure any profit at the outset. You will have done calculations to ensure that the yield is at least 8% and the property will generate cashflow and passive income. Now, capital growth is a bonus to the initial investment.

So, to repeat: do your homework, buy *below* market value to make the initial profit.

For now, though, we are simply interested in how we account for the rental income; we'll revisit issues such as capital growth and potential capital gains later.

As an investor, rental income is accounted for on an annual basis to 5 April each year, less the expenses incurred during that year. When a property investor decides to dispose of a property then that disposal will be treated as a capital gain. The investor *may* be able to make use of what is called the 'annual exemption' – and I say *may* because, if the investor has disposed of other capital assets (such as shares or even a piece of furniture) this exemption might have been used elsewhere.

This annual exemption, as its name suggests, is available each year to every individual. Current rates are available on the HMRC website; for the 2013/14 tax year this is £10,600, per person: so a jointly-held property could show a healthy profit of around £21,000 with no Capital Gains Tax payable.

Issues for a property investor to consider will include:

- Rental profit and loss accounts must be produced annually, with any profit taxed at your marginal rate of tax

- Capital profit is subject to Capital Gains Tax

- Use of annual Capital Gains Tax exemption

- Possible use of principal private residence relief (PPR) (this is discussed later)

- Capital gains will be totally exempt for non-UK residents

- No National Insurance will be payable on profits.

However, the tax regime is less forgiving for certain types of abortive expenditure. For example, if you are busy buying property through auctions and always get a full survey, the costs of the survey and any legal fees would only be allowable *if you actually purchased the property*. All other surveys, for which your properties your bids were unsuccessful, would be a lost expense to a property investor. Yes, that seems wrong. But that's the law of the land and nobody said that the tax laws had to fair or indeed equitable!

3.3 So what about a property trader?

A property *trader* will purchase a property with a view to making a profit and not holding the asset long term as an investment. That profit may be through a simple refurbishment of a tired and dated property, possibly splitting it into flats, adding rooms whatever and then selling the property on or "flipping it". A trader is very unlikely to ever let that property (though circumstances may conspire against him so that he is forced to let that property) and the profit is made when the property is sold on for a higher price.

The property trader could be trading in his own name (as a sole trader); with a business partner (in a partnership); or through a limited company (ltd) or a limited liability partnership (LLP). Here, any profit would be subject to Income Tax and National Insurance – or Corporation Tax, if held within a limited company.

Some of the things that a property trader needs to be aware of will include:

- Better scope for claiming abortive expenditure

- No use of annual exemption for Capital Gains Tax

- Greater relief for interest costs

- Ability to choose any year end

- Losses used against other income

- Profits taxed at marginal rates and attract National Insurance, if self-employed

- Profits charged to corporation tax, if a limited company.

So, given the tax treatment, it may be becoming clear why people want to call themselves investors when they might be traders – or vice versa. The big question will always be whether any profit is a *capital gain* or a *trading profit*.

This distinction is not clear-cut and naturally keeps HMRC on their toes, looking for traders who want to be investors and occasionally investors who might think they want to be traders. Investors who should have been classed as traders will typically provide HMRC with more tax   revenue – both in terms of the higher rates of income tax and the potential penalties that may be imposed, once they are identified. So HMRC are targeting those where there is a blurring of the boundaries.

3.4 So am I an investor or a trader?

Regrettably it is not your choice! As indicated at the start of the chapter, the answer to this question is determined by (a) how the business is run and (b) on your intentions at the outset. As you presumably made clear to your partner, your intentions were honourable and made evident, early on in your relationship. Property is no different and HMRC will look to your intentions when you bought the property.

In simple terms, if you intend to buy this property at auction, add value and then sell it on – then chances are that you are a trader. If you intend to buy this property at auction, add value, let out and then remortgage in six months to get your initial cash deposit back, chances are that you are an investor.

Ok, so that's crystal clear. But how do you prove your intentions to HMRC? And what if you change your mind?

What can you do to ensure that you don't find yourself being treated as a trader when, in reality, you are an investor:

- Start with making a note as to why you bought a property. Maybe write to your accountant, explaining what you are doing and what your intentions are with the property. That should, in itself, cause them to ask further questions; if they are proactive and take an interest in your affairs they could possibly prevent you from stumbling into a tax minefield. If, for whatever reason, you chose to deal with your own tax affairs then maybe send a note to your solicitor.

- We all know that 'failing to plan is planning to fail' and I'm sure that readers of this book will have planned their investment strategy but, if needed, a business plan would also demonstrate what your plans were.

- If, for some reason, plans change – then document them as well. There may be a perfectly good reason why a long-term investment was sold short term and documentary proof will help you argue your case with HMRC. Your long-term investment in a student flat in Cambridge could swiftly move from long term to short term if little Jimmy stuffs his A levels and ends up somewhere less academic or, indeed, decides he doesn't fancy university after all.

- Be very wary about the *frequency* of transactions. If a property is bought and sold every now and then, that would suggest an investor; if you are buying frequently and selling on, that would suggest a trader.

- HMRC also get quite excited about the *number of transactions in a given period*. In theory there is nothing to stop you buying a house, improving it and moving on and making full use of the Principal Private Residence exemption (more later on this). Do this every six months and HMRC may get excited and would suggest property trading. After all, moving is one of the most stressful things you can do – so why would you choose to do it every six months?

- How are you *financing* your transactions? Mortgages and long-term finance are more indicative of investment, though nowadays some see an early repayment charge when you redeem a mortgage early as part of development costs!

- *Letting out* a property is indicative of an investment not a trade.

- The *duration* of your holding a property may also influence HMRC though, again, there is no hard-and-fast rule on this one.

So, in summary, call yourself what you like – *Supreme Allied Property Developer* or *Joint Chief of Staff* – but remember that your *intentions* and *actions* will determine whether HMRC see you as a property investor or property trader.

Get that right and you will keep a lot of money out of the taxman's hands.

Of course you may be both a property investor and a trader, in which case you may need different trading vehicles and throughout the book I will explain how this works.

Tax Tip

Be crystal clear about what your intentions are when buying a property, so as not to find yourself exposed to the wrong taxes.

CHAPTER 4

Property Taxes:
Common Areas for Investors and Traders

4.1 Introduction

Once you have established whether you are a property investment business or a property trading business there are some areas of common ground, mainly to do with expenses and some aspects unique to each.

So let's go through all the common areas first and then expand in later chapters as appropriate to drill down on the key areas for an investor or a trader.

At its simplest, if an item of expenditure is incurred within your business (from a simple postage stamp to a full refurbishment of your property) then it can be claimed or set against your taxable profit, though there are some underlying principles that need to be set out at the start.

The 'revenue' v 'capital' debate

In any business, expenditure is either capital or revenue. *Revenue* expenditure can be deducted from your income. To be claimed as an expense, then it must be incurred, usually but not necessarily, on an annual basis with the intention of earning revenue.

Capital expenditure, on the other hand, is not deducted from your income. Instead, that expenditure is carried forward with a deduction allowed when you come to sell the property. Just to confuse you slightly, *some* capital expenditure can be offset against your income through what are called 'capital allowances' or 'wear and tear allowances'.

Don't worry, these will all be covered to ensure that you won't miss out!

At its most basic, buying the property is *capital* expenditure; expenses in running the property are *revenue* expenditure. But as inflation erodes the real value of expenditure incurred today, the objective is to achieve deductions now rather than let inflation erode the real value of that money. Besides, you may never sell – so you will never get the benefit of that deduction.

Whether the expenditure is a capital or revenue expense will also depend on the kind of business that you have and this will get explained later. As you can imagine in property this distinction is very important; it can save – or cost – you an awful lot of tax.

Wholly & exclusively

All tax inspectors (and even some accountants) get very excited about this phrase, which to a civil servant is almost their holy creed.

The legislation disallows any expenditure not incurred *wholly and exclusively* for the purposes of the trade, profession or vocation. This means that the rule is only satisfied if the taxpayer's sole purpose for incurring the expense is for the purposes of their trade, profession or vocation.

Not being risk takers, the taxman doesn't understand that, to earn a pound, you might have to spend a few first; they certainly wouldn't want you to benefit from that expenditure. So, as taxpayers, we need to worry about mixed use and dual purpose.

A *mixed use* is where you might buy a newspaper for its detailed and informative property section (most of the quality weekend papers have these). Your eyes might then wander to the news or even sport sections – but because the purpose was to look at the property section then this will not fail the wholly and exclusive test. If you had an anorak or maybe two you could possibly apportion the private element.

Dual-purpose expenditure is expenditure that is incurred for more than one reason. If one of the reasons is not for business purposes, the expenditure fails; there is no provision that allows a 'business' proportion. I need to wear clothes, for example; they may be worn during my property-investing activities but I need to wear clothes anyway so there is no tax deduction.

Tax Tip

Purchase suitably branded work wear, swear shirts, protective clothing, etc. and claim a full deduction.

4.2 Loan Interest and Finance Charges

You would be amazed at the tax relief that can be obtained on your borrowings and interest. Interest is an allowable expense and whilst, on the face of it, you would think it fairly straightforward where interest would be claimed you may be leaving some expenses on the HMRC table.

Essentially loan interest is allowable on:

- Capital which has been introduced into the property business

- Other funds that have been used within the property business.

Let's look at each in turn.

Capital into the business

When a property first enters the letting market the value of that property at that time represents capital which has been introduced into the business. In addition, any other costs incurred in bringing that property to the market (such as stamp duty, legal fees, repairs, etc.) will be allowable, so any interest incurred in meeting those capital costs should be claimed against your profits.

Dallaglio had a property in which he lived, with a great deal of equity; he only had a small mortgage of £50,000.

He wanted to move and let his house out (there are loads of reliefs to come later with your main home in the Capital Gains Tax chapter) but for now let's concentrate on the interest charge.

His house was worth £200,000, so he borrowed a further £100,000; this meant that he now had allowable borrowings of £150,000. The value of that property was £200,000 when it entered the lettings market and the amount of borrowings was £150,000.

He has two choices:

1. *He could spend the £100,000 on buying more houses and clearly that would qualify for tax relief in its own right*

2. *If he so desired, he could cruise the world or buy a fast new car and still obtain tax relief on that additional debt.*

In either situation he will obtain tax relief on the interest paid because the value of the new debt £100,000 was in situ when the property first entered the lettings market.

Tax Tip

Maximise the good debt on an asset before it enters the lettings market; if you have to, use some of that good debt to clear the expensive bad debt of credit card liabilities.

A more traditional approach but nonetheless equally relevant is as follows:

King Richard Hill buys a house for £100,000 which he knows is well below market value. With a 75% buy-to-let mortgage he will obtain tax relief on his borrowings of £75,000.

All the usual work is undertaken to add value (and yes, we will cover the tax aspect of repairs) and after six months he looks to remortgage the property. The surveyor attends and, because he is having a good day, has not had a row with his other half and is feeling positive about life he values the property correctly at £130,000.

Pleased as punch, King Hill then borrows 75% of the £130,000, getting full tax relief on the interest paid on borrowings of £97,500. Note that this is still below the capital value of the property when it entered the lettings market. After repaying the original mortgage, taking account of legals and borrowing fees, King Hill is perfectly free to spend the extra cash released on what he wants. However, being a savvy property investor, he recycles the cash into another property.

Let's roll the clock forward, say ten years, and assume that the doom and gloom is behind us and that the property is now worth £200,000. King Hill wants to release some of the equity in the property. Well 75% of £200,000 is £150,000 so what borrowings will qualify for tax relief?

Initially it will be 100/150ths: the 100 being the initial value when it entered the market and the 150 being the value of borrowings now. Yes,

King Hill can do what he likes with the money – but he will need to apportion the interest charge.

Or does he? If King Hill uses those funds in the property business, maybe to provide working capital, pay for training or on-going running costs, then the money spent here will enable the debt to qualify for tax relief. Equally, if as above the funds are rolled over and used to provide money to put down as a deposit for a new investment property, then tax relief will be given on the interest.

Tax Tip

You will begin to see that you will need to keep careful records (spread sheets usually work best) of where the cash released ultimately was spent; but there is no reason why careful record keeping will not prevent one of the biggest expenses, namely loan interest, being 100% tax deductible.

Other funds used in the business

Providing working capital to your business is where interest qualifies in the second category but it need not be from remortgaged property.

These days nearly everybody makes a purchase on a credit card, so why not have one card used solely for your property business. In the event that you can't pay off the bill in full then the penal amount of interest that the credit card company charges is an allowable expense.

Back uses a dedicated credit card so that there can be no dispute that the interest charged is for the property business. If you stick in groceries and other personal living expenses then such interest will need to be apportioned and, while it can be done, that's time consuming and not a good use of your or your accountant's time.

Tax Tip

Use a dedicated credit card for business and if unable to clear the debt for whatever reason the interest will be tax deductible.

If you have managed to secure a bank overdraft for your business, then congratulations are in order. They were what banks used to give to customers to help them grow their business. So if you have one, treasure and nurture it; all interest and costs associated with this will be allowable, even the charges applied and the punitive fixed fee they charge you simply to write to you and renew the overdraft.

More likely, in the absence of a sympathetic bank manager, you sourced a personal loan or joint venture finance; if the funds were used in your business, maybe to pay for training or to a builder, then please claim the interest paid.

The final area that we need to look at under finance is *loan arrangement fees* and the impact of *early redemption fees*.

Loan fees will typically be written off over the period of the loan. So you have secured a great loan interest rate but the lender has loaded the fees over the 20-year borrowings. So write off 1/20th of the fees each year and in the year that you move the mortgage then claim the balance of those fees in full

Slattery borrowed £75,000 interest only over a 20-year period. It had a good initial rate fixed for three years but a fee of 3% £2,250. In each tax year Slattery claimed £112.50 against the property rental income. After three years the loan was switched to a new product and yes there were lending fees again but in that year we could claim the remaining amount of the lending fees in full.

In the above example there was no early repayment charge but if there had been could it be claimed as an allowable expense?

I would always say yes as the change in borrowing was a commercial decision. You wanted to move to a better interest rate, release capital to go investing again though strangely HMRC treat these as personal costs.

Tax Tip

As I've said elsewhere if you document why you switched and can clearly demonstrate that it was a business decision then continue to claim early repayment charges on your tax return.

4.3 Legal Fees

We all know that sharks don't eat solicitors out of professional courtesy but, love them or hate them, you will need to use them during your property investing career. Yes, you can do your own conveyancing but ask yourself if that is really a good use of your time.

Concentrate on your key skills and buy in expertise where needed. The one thing everyone has in this life that is equal is the 24 hours in a day – so use *your* 24 on what you are most good at and leverage other people's skill and time. Does Richard Branson fly his own planes? Does Duncan Bannatyne open up the gym every morning? You catch my drift, so find and use your solicitor and make use of or leverage his expertise.

So, are legal fees *capital* or *revenue* expenditure? Your first encounter will be when you buy the property. Legal costs in acquiring the property cannot be claimed against your rental income; they will be treated as a capital expense and, thus, carried forward.

All is not lost however. Within the conveyancing process, part of the legal work will relate to the raising of the finance and the solicitor helpfully telling you that you are borrowing at x% and that your home can be repossessed ... (all the stuff that, as a wise property investor, you already knew). So ask you solicitor how much of the bill related to raising the finance and then claim that part as *revenue expenditure*.

Tax Tip

Ask for a separate bill or a clear indication of what costs have been incurred in dealing with the finance and claim against your income.

After speaking at a property event in 2012, somebody came to me and asked about this. He was appalled to learn that his accountant had not done this and he had over fifty properties. Fifty properties, at say £150 per property, amounts to £7,500 expenditure treated as capital expenditure and not revenue expenditure; with his marginal rate of tax at 50%, that represented £3,750 tax that he could have saved. Ouch!

In addition, where tenants fall behind and you have to bring any form of legal action, then those costs will always be allowable.

4.4 Other Professional Fees

It's not just the legal profession that wants a chunk of your hard-earned income – and, again, it is important to distinguish between capital and revenue expenditure.

When buying the property, as well as the legal fees, you will incur survey fees, maybe a finder's fee and valuation fees. All of these will need to be treated as *capital expenditure*: they are part of the cost of acquiring the property. Tax relief is ultimately given when the property is eventually disposed of. (Just to confuse matters slightly, once you have the property any costs in *remortgaging* the property would be treated as revenue, not capital expenditure.)

Letting fees paid to agents will be allowable, as will the fees paid to your accountant for sorting out your tax return or completing your annual accounts.

Choose professional people to work with in your property business carefully. As indicated above with solicitors, all professional fees should be an excellent use of your money and time. Use their expertise and leverage it to your advantage. But do remember that, to an extent, your 'purchase' of professional services is no different to purchasing a packet of cornflakes or a new camera.

By that I mean that there are independent financial advisors (IFAs), solicitors, accountants (be they chartered, certified or even unqualified) and letting agents throughout the land – all of whom can do what you require. None of them will ever say "we're not very good" or "we have no experience of property investing". Unless they are actively involved in your specific sector, they will not necessarily ask the right questions. These days the world is a much smaller place so location is less of an issue, but specialism is so important.

So please choose very wisely:

- Don't go to a generalist: I wouldn't go to a liver specialist to get my heart looked and nor a heart surgeon to sort my liver

- Ideally, ensure that they also invest in property – so that they will clearly understand your needs

- Appoint someone you know like and trust; absolutely essential

- Does your accountant demonstrate that they can save more than they charge

- Always agree a fixed fee in advance

- See these expenses as an *investment*, not a *cost*.

Why do I talk about 'investment' and 'cost'? Well, I'm reminded of the lady who calls out the plumber because the central heating system is rattling and keeping the family awake at night. Exasperated, she calls out a professional to sort this out, a plumber. He arrives, checks out a few things, opens the tool box and removes a large club hammer. He hits the boiler three times and the noise stops. "Thank you," says the lady. "You must send me your bill."

The following day a bill arrives and the narration reads 'Fixing central heating system: fee £500'. Somewhat aggrieved, the lady phones up and demands an amended bill. The following day a new bill duly arrives: 'Hitting boiler with hammer £1; Knowing where to hit boiler, £499. Total fee: £500'.

Expertise really is well worth paying for.

4.5 Abortive Costs

Finally in this section on professional fees we need to look at how the tax dice roll when things don't quite go your way.

- You've found the ideal property, searches ordered, solicitors instructed, etc. – and then, for whatever reason, the purchase falls through. Having gnashed teeth, grumbled to the agent and dusted yourself down you've incurred abortive costs! Here's a tax unfairness coming, and I know not why, but if you run a property *investment* business you just have to take those costs on the chin. There will be no deduction to be included in your Income Tax Return.

- If on the other hand you were running a property *trading* business then those costs are all part of the everyday expenditure and thus allowable.

- You've found the ideal property and had a survey done which reveals more work required than your initial inspection (remember leveraging) so you decide not to proceed. This may be an allowable expense, see criteria above, or one to have to take on the chin.

Tax Tip

If you are in the habit of taking educated punts on auction purchases, then you really should be a property *trader* and not an investor otherwise these abortive cost can become significant; with no tax relief they can be very expensive!

4.6 Training and Education

In 1985 when I bought my first house I enjoyed my first period of on-the-job property investment training. I knew nothing and as you can imagine the learning curve was pretty steep:

- What language were the surveyors speaking

- What did all that legal jargon mean

- Was I to go interest-free or repayment

- Did I need an endowment

- What vehicle did I have in place to repay...

These were just some of the daunting challenges that, like you, I faced with my first house purchase. Nine months, later when I sold it for £10,000 more than I paid for it, I thought I knew all I needed to know about property and could call myself a property investor!

Clearly that isn't the case. The property market, like any market, is constantly changing and there is always a need to keep up to date with current trends and industry thinking. So yes, I continue to invest in my education. Can these costs be claimed? Absolutely – but there is a catch, as HMRC deem that education and learning of a new skill are not allowable. Why, I know not. If I were a perfectly capable electrician, and thought that I wanted to train to be a plumber, those costs would be deemed to be a personal and not a business expense!

So how does that work with a new property investor?

Well, pay to acquire some basic property investment knowledge, remembering that these are your own costs - you can't reclaim them, so keep them low at this stage. A book is probably the cheapest way: the Ladybird Book of Property Investing would be a good place to start if it existed, but there are plenty of books to get you started. Once you've understood the basics, and maybe attended a property networking event, then I reckon you are up and running. You have the knowledge to invest.

Providing that it is a book relevant to the subject and gives you a basic understanding of how investment property works, then you can know call yourself a property investor. Any future education will be building on that initial training investment that you paid for yourself.

Any subsequent training will be an allowable expense. If you want to enhance your knowledge about lease options or maybe deal packaging then do so – and claim the cost and all associated costs (see later).

Incidentally, be prepared to argue this point with your accountant – as some appear to work for HMRC! A client came to me because her then accountant was not allowing her to claim property education costs and quoting HMRC manuals at her. This person had been investing in property for over five years so it's fair to assume that she was not a newbie to property investing.

Tax Tip

Build on your knowledge and get 100% tax relief by claiming all the costs and keep a record of your initial privately-funded training.

4.7 Books, Magazines and Journals

As indicated above, the first book to gain new knowledge must be treated as a personal expense. Thereafter, claim for anything and everything that furthers your knowledge.

To take an appalling legal advert that says "where there's a blame, there's a claim", think "where there's an expense there's a claim".

So books to further your negotiation skills with vendors, books to enhance your selling skills, and, yes, even books on personal development, how to deal package, newspapers, journals forums etc. Make a note and keep a record of the expenditure and make a claim.

Some of you may think well it's not worth the effort. If that's the case, lucky you but if you spend £1 on a Friday to buy the *Times* for its property section and £2.50 for the *Sunday Times* (there are other papers available and online editions) that's £182 a year. If you are a higher rate taxpayer that represents £82 tax saved and put in your pocket. That's enough to fund a weekend away exploring possible investment opportunities (which you might also be able to claim for!).

Can I thank you for investing in this book; I trust that you have found, and will continue to find, many ways to avoid and thus save tax – but please, please, ensure that you have included the cost within your monthly expenses.

> ## Tax Tip
>
> **Keep all newspaper and book receipts and claim against your rental income.**

4.8 Travel and Subsistence

This is another area where many people, especially your accountant, will leave money on the revenue's table. You would be amazed how many miles you travel as a property investor, so it's essential that you make a claim for all those miles travelled.

Some of you invest in areas well away from where you live as the yields in your area don't stack up. So if you find yourself hurtling down the M4 to Wales, or heading up the M1 to the frozen north (it's not really, it's just wonderful) to undertake viewings – then be sure to keep a record of the mileage undertaken. Just think how many times you will clock up mileage: attending viewings, a trip to the auction house, a visit to your IFA, a visit to your solicitor, your friendly accountant, networking events, training events. Those wonderful miles can then be claimed at 45p (2013/14) for the first 10,000 and 25p thereafter. These rates do change, and the current claimable amount can be found here:

http://www.hmrc.gov.uk/rates/travel.htm

> ## Tax Tip
>
> **Keep a diary for an average month and you would be amazed at the miles undertaken. A simple multiplication times 12 would give you a typical annual mileage on which to make a claim. If you have an anorak, or maybe work for HMRC, then you would dutifully record every trip, 365 days of the year. Yes, the second method will be 100% correct but the former will be a good approximation and a quicker, more commercial, approach.**

There is now an app called "Trip Cubby" that records daily mileage, so you've now no excuse for not claiming all relevant mileage at the correct rate.

When I was speaking at a presentation, someone put their hand up and said that her accountant claims a proportion of her whole car expenses. That is an equally acceptable way of doing it; you take your 'property miles' as a percentage of your 'total miles travelled' and apply that percentage to your total motor vehicle expenses.

Both work, but in my experience the mileage route works best - and certainly requires less record-keeping. I suggested that she kept a record for two months of her property mileage and compared that to a percentage of her motor running costs. She was surprised at just how many property miles that she did and the fact that her claim was much higher than a simple percentage of the total running costs for those two months.

As I said, both work: it is for you to decide which way to claim.

As you travel the length and breadth of this country by car, whether viewing properties or attending events, you might need to eat and drink to stay alive. Can you claim for that as well? As that annoying little dog says, "Oh yes!" – but be *reasonable* and be *sensible*.

If you feel the need for a skinny latte, a bottle of water, a BLT or egg and cress then keep the receipt and claim the expense. If you stay away, then again claim for the hotel expense and, yes, the evening meal as well. If you find yourself in deepest Peterborough attending a training event (who on earth could that be with?) you will need to feed and water yourself, so claim for that curry and a pint or two because it's allowable.

You need to eat and drink to survive and you are doing no more than you would at home – but the fact that you are away from home means that you have to incur *additional* expense and thus it's allowable. Equally, if you are attending a networking event and it is a *better use of your time* to stay overnight then claim for it. But, as ever please, don't go mad! Don't claim for twelve pints of lager and packet of crisps nor nip into Le

Gavroche when in London as you needed a bite to eat. Unless of course you can demonstrate that your *normal* style is to be staying in five-star hotels, it is probably not acceptable to book into the Ritz if there are cheaper hotels nearby.

My motto with every legitimate expense is "Rip it, but don't tear it!"

If you take your partner with you then if they are actively involved in the property business then claim for them as well or if not just claim a proportion.

Other travel expenses that should be claimed will be train and underground fares, taxis, flights, car parking – even bus fares if you use that method of transport! I tend to travel a lot by train and usually first class; not because I can, but because it ensures that I can double up on the use of my time. While the driver takes me there, apart from the intrusion of the ticket collector and the odd free coffee (sometimes very odd) there's some 'net extra time' to read a book, further my education or do some work.

By 'net extra time' I mean that the three hours travelling have also given me three hours to learn, so I've effectively got six hours out of three. Equally, if I have to take the car I will ensure that I'm listening to something thought-provoking that will help me take the business forward, though late-night drives home lend themselves to music and a chance to put the pedal down.

What about overseas travel?

Some care needs to be applied when you venture overseas and that's just not to make sure some pickpocket doesn't disappear with your wallet, as happened to me once in Paris: talk about the quickest way to ruin an overseas trip.

No, the care that needs to be applied is that travel subsistence and accommodation costs will only be allowable if the trip was *purely* for business. So, if you travel to Spain for a long weekend because, having done your research at home, you genuinely think that Spain is the place to invest, then all expenses relating to that trip will be allowable, despite the fact that after two days viewing houses, meeting agents you took yourself down to the seafront, had two glasses of San Miguel and caught a couple of hours of sun.

However, if you took the whole family away to the Costa Brava and idly wandered into an estate agent to enquire about property then, not surprisingly, the whole trip would be deemed to be personal, not business.

If, on the other hand, you can clearly demonstrate that there was a business element (perhaps because you already own property over there and were meeting with agents, bankers or whoever) then Dad or Mum's proportion or even both could be claimed. Again be proportional and sensible.

Tax Tip

Get in the habit or recording all travel and subsistence expenditure, and the reason for it – and enjoy the tax relief.

4.9 Capital allowances

Plant & Machinery

Whether you are in business as a trader or an investor, then you can claim tax allowances, also known as capital allowances, on certain purchases or investments that you make on business assets. You cannot *directly* deduct your expenditure on those assets by including the cost in the profit and loss account; instead you can deduct a 'capital allowance'. This applies whether you're self-employed and pay Income Tax, or are a company or organisation that's liable for Corporation Tax. Many common business assets, such as office equipment, furniture and machines or tools, may be considered to be plant and machinery for capital allowance purposes; expenditure on them might qualify for plant and machinery allowances. You can, in certain circumstances, claim capital allowances for capital expenditure on specific types of building improvement and renovation. As with all capital allowances, there are conditions that have to be met before you can claim them. This is particularly relevant for those with the following:

- Commercial property

- Houses of multiple occupancy (HMOs)

- Furnished lettings

- Caravan parks.

Apart from the allowances described here, capital allowances are generally not available for expenditure on land or buildings.

Items that qualify for plant and machinery allowances will include, but are not restricted to, tools, machinery, vehicles and other equipment you own (having bought them for your business). There are also certain fixtures in buildings, and integral features in buildings, that qualify for plant and machinery allowances.

Rules for plant and machinery allowances

To qualify for plant and machinery allowances, all the following must apply:

1. You must have incurred capital expenditure on the provision of plant and machinery that is used wholly or partly for the purposes of your business. You must own the asset in question as a result of incurring that expenditure

2. The asset must not be something you buy and sell by way of

your trade, although you might eventually sell it for some other reason - you may then have to make an adjustment to your capital allowances. The asset must also not get used up in producing what you sell or supply by way of your trade

3. The asset must generally be expected to last for more than two years. It's also worth discussing here the concept of materiality. A portable concrete mixer may well last for more than two years but, in reality, like most items these are really now a disposable item; the cost would be written off within repairs. In any business, capital expenditure below £500 should be written off; as the size of the business grows, that figure show be increased.

If you *partly* use an asset for non-business use, you can still claim capital allowances on the business use of the asset. The allowances you claim must be reduced by the amount arising out of your non-business use so that only the business proportion is taken into account. So if you've a van that you use for business and personal use and are not claiming the business mileage, then you can restrict the claim by that percentage of private mileage.

Fixtures in buildings

You may be able to claim plant and machinery allowances for expenditure on certain fixtures in a building that is in use for the purposes of your business. This expenditure qualifies for writing-down allowances. All the capital expenditure is combined in a "pool". The rate for the main pool is, currently 20 per cent. Qualifying fixtures can include:

- Some kitchen equipment

- Bathroom suites, and some fittings

- Fire alarm systems

- CCTV

- Burglar alarm systems.

Note that if your business is an ordinary UK property business (i.e. single lets) you can't claim capital allowances for expenditure on plant or machinery (including those that are fixtures or integral features), for use within a dwelling house that you rent out. However, expenditure on plant or machinery for use within common parts of a building that contains more than one dwelling may qualify.

Integral features of buildings

You can claim plant and machinery allowances for expenditure on certain, specified assets called integral features of a building or structure that is in use for the purposes of your business. Expenditure on integral features qualifies for writing down allowance at the rate for the special rate pool (currently 8 per cent.)

- The following are integral features:

- Electrical systems, including lighting systems

- Cold water systems

- Space or water heating systems, powered systems of ventilation, air cooling or air purification, and any floor or ceiling comprised in such systems

- Lifts, escalators, and moving walkways

- External solar heating.

You would be amazed how certain buildings are stuffed with expenditure waiting for capital allowances to be claimed but these have been missed by investors' accountants because this is such a specialist area.

Tax Tip

If you own and have purchased within the last ten years a commercial building, HMO, caravan park or furnished lettings, appoint a specialist to identify areas of expenditure that will attract those capital allowances.

Typically, up to 25% of the purchase costs of the freehold property, across a wide spectrum of commercial buildings, can be claimed.

If would like to enquire further please email Iain @iainwallis.com. There's a nominal initial commitment fee which is fully refunded if my team don't identify a potential claim so this really is a no-risk purchase.

Tax Tip

Recent changes in tax legislation regarding fixtures in commercial properties mean that, if you decide to sell your property after April 2014 and have not previously claimed all capital allowances on the fixtures, you will be required to identify and pool all the qualifying fixtures, separating out integral features, whether you have claimed for these or not. So, like all good scouts, "Be Prepared" when you are asked for this information as part of the sale contract.

Types of plant and machinery allowances

There are a number of allowances available for expenditure on plant and machinery.

Annual Investment Allowance

Most businesses can claim an Annual Investment Allowance for expenditure on most plant and machinery, apart from cars. In many cases (depending on your level of expenditure) this may mean that you can claim your entire expenditure on qualifying items against this allowance. The annual amount of Annual Investment Allowance was £25,000 though there has been a temporary increase of the annual amount from £25,000 to £250,000, for two years, in relation to expenditure incurred on or after 1 January 2013.

Currently, there are 100 per cent first-year allowances available for expenditure on certain specific types of asset. This means you can claim the full expenditure on these assets as a deduction when calculating your taxable profit or loss for the accounting period when you spent the money, if all the conditions are met.

The key types of assets, some of which may be relevant in your property business, that qualify for first-year allowances are:

- New, unused cars with CO_2 emissions of not more than 110 grams per kilometre driven

- Certain designated energy-efficient equipment

- Certain environmentally beneficial, currently water-efficient equipment

- Equipment for refuelling vehicles with natural gas, biogas or hydrogen fuel

- New zero-emission goods vehicles, such as electric vans.

Tax Tip

Note that the annual investment allowance is personal to you. Two people holding an investment properties jointly (but not within a formal business partnership) will each be entitled to their own annual investment allowance.

Writing-down allowances (WDA)

Writing-down allowances are annual allowances that reduce, or 'write down' any balance of capital expenditure on plant and machinery that you haven't been able to claim (either the annual investment allowance or a first-year allowance), and on residual balances of expenditure that you have carried forward from the previous accounting period.

There are two rates of WDA for plant and machinery. To calculate them, you first group your expenditure into different 'pools':

- The main pool: this includes expenditure on most items - the rate is 18 per cent

- The special rate pool: this includes special rate expenditure, including long-life assets, integral features, certain thermal insulation and some cars - the rate is 8 per cent.

Writing-down allowances for expenditure on short-life assets, or assets that you have used partly for non-business purposes, are calculated individually. That expenditure is therefore added into a separate pool for each asset, known as a 'single asset pool'. A business may have several single asset pools. The rate of writing-down allowance to apply to each pool will depend on the type of asset on which the expenditure was incurred.

Small pools allowance

If, in either the main or special rate pool, the remaining balance is £1,000 or less after you have carried out the steps, then instead of claiming a percentage writing-down allowance you can claim an allowance, sometimes called the Special Pools Allowance (SPA), for the whole amount remaining in that pool.

Tax Tip

At lower levels of profit it may be that your personal allowance exceeds the level of profit. In which case don't claim the capital allowances as they will be wasted and carry forward to when you need them to reduce your taxable profit.

4.10 Other Admin Expenses

Most of you would, I guess, be working from home – maybe from a dedicated office – and it would be remiss not to claim for relevant costs as a legitimate business expense. After all, if you had a town centre office, you could claim all of that - so by working from home you are actually charging less to HMRC than you, potentially, could!

Typically, you would take a proportion based on the number of rooms in the house, excluding the kitchen, bathrooms, hall, stairs and landing. So, if you are working from a simple two-up, two-down house, and using one bedroom as an office this would mean you could claim 25% of the household bills as a business expense.

Always ensure that there is some private element as well, whether that be from guests visiting or other non-business use (the ironing room is always good) and typically this will not exceed 10%, which means you are limiting your base cost to only 90% of the total. Why?

Well, it demonstrates that you are a reasonable person and have considered the private element but, more importantly, when you come to sell the home it will prevent HMRC from claiming a proportion of that tax-free gain as their own. (In practice, this may well be covered by other exemptions but just be aware of that fact.)

So you can claim 22.5% (25% home × 90% usage) of household bills, which will include:

- Council tax

- General repairs to the house

- Insurance

- Mortgage interest

- Light & heat.

Tax Tip

Set yourself up a spreadsheet to record all the household expenses and make a legitimate claim based on a reasonably and sensible business proportion.

Other admin costs that can all be claimed will be the phone, the mobile, the internet – with a suitable private use adjustment. By a private use adjustment you will apportion any bill between private and business usage. Don't forget all printing postage and stationery, computer consumables, etc. The list of what you can claim for really is endless.

Other Deductions

Don't forget to claim for these costs where appropriate:

- Ground rents and service charges, if you invest in flats

- Gardeners, if you provide them

- Cleaners (especially holiday lettings and rent-to-rent)

- Agents' commission and tenant finders' fees

- Property adverts, if you self-manage

- Light and heat during voids

- Council tax during voids.

Most if not all local councils have removed the six-month exemption where the property is empty. The fact that the six-month void for empty property has now been removed should encourage all of us to be exceedingly efficient with refurbishments and remember to also bring these costs into the budgets at the start, and also ensure that the property is marketed so that tenants move in as soon as the carpet has been laid and the property deep-cleaned.

4.11 Pre-Trading Expenditure

When you finally land your first investment property it may be after a long and, sometimes, a weary search. So the good news is that all the pre-trading expenditure incurred in your property business (provided that, in the normal course of events, they are deductible expenses) can be claimed as if the money was spent on day one. So, from the moment you set out on your property journey, be sure to start recording all those expenses. You can actually claim for expenditure incurred in the previous seven years – but hopefully it won't take you that long to source your first property!

Tax Tip

The moment you start out on your property investing journey, start keeping a record of your expenditure and this book will help you identify what to record.

4.12 VAT

We cover this in a later chapter and look at where and when you can recover this tax. To the extent that you are unable to recover the VAT then it just makes the expense more expensive to you as the end user.

4.13 Year-end Planning

In any business, the year end offers a fantastic opportunity to plan your tax affairs in the most beneficial way. At its simplest we want to bring forward expenditure, be that capital or revenue, and defer income – but always mindful that the tax tail must not wag the commercial dog.

Rates of tax change from year to year, so you might want to defer income – or bring it forward. There was a massive spike in bonuses and dividends paid in 2009/10, prior to the introduction of the 50% additional tax rate; and a spike in early April 2013 when the higher rate reduced to 45% in 2013/14. Proof, were it needed, that the high earners manage their tax affairs so whilst politically the 50% rate may have been popular – it actually cost UK Plc. tax revenue!

I will give specific examples when we look at investors and traders but, for now, consider these means of changing the date when you incur expenditure:

- If not already used up, spend your annual investment allowance

- Get contracts in place for large repair projects

- Accrue bonuses for staff and or directors (make sure that they get paid within nine months of the year end)

- Bring forward replacement of capital items in furnished lettings properties were you are not claiming the 10% wear and tear allowance.

It's difficult, if not impossible, to defer rental *income* – but if you are about to sell a property that you've held as an asset, delaying that completion by just a few days could buy you twelve months to pay that tax. Equally, if you are a trader and flipping, it is always best to do just after – and not just before – your year end.

With that all behind us let's now look at the specifics for property investors and traders.

> ## Tax Tip
>
> **Wherever possible bring forward expenditure and defer income to gain a cashflow advantage.**

CHAPTER 5

Avoiding Taxes in a Property Investment Business

5.1 Introduction

So we've run through the areas where expenditure and the underlying principles will overlap, so let's look at specifics for those in the property *investment* business. Just to remind you, that here you are buying an investment to hold for the medium to long term, with the expectation of receiving monthly rental income.

You will need to prepare a simple income & expenditure account for each property and then combine these for one entry onto your self-assessment return.

You will also, if you have them, need to account separately for:

- Qualified furnished holiday lettings

- Overseas lettings.

However tempting it may seem, **all** rental income must be declared; even more importantly, just because you have not made a profit don't think that you can ignore HMRC, so – if you haven't already done so – you will need to visit the HMRC website and obtain what is called your 'Unique Taxpayers Reference' or, more snappily, your UTR. You can do this here:

http://www.hmrc.gov.uk/sa/register.htm

You need to submit your return:

a) To get the losses agreed and carried forward to subsequent years

b) More importantly to declare a source of income, even if this is an unprofitable one at this stage.

Not to do so will put you at the mercy of HMRC who, having scoured the land registry's files, are interested to know why your name appears on the title deeds but you haven't filed a return.

> ## Tax Tip
>
> **Register with HMRC before they find you!**

You will need to draw accounts up to 5 April each tax year; they will be prepared on what accountants call an 'accruals' basis – or, put more simply, income and expenditure is recognised when it arises or incurred, not when money enters or leaves the bank account.

Just to confuse matters, if your gross rental receipts do not exceed £15,000 you can prepare accounts on a simpler cash basis (i.e. money in, less money out).

Your self-assessment return can be filed by paper or online by one of two dates after the year that is being assessed. If you choose to file a paper return it **must** reach HMRC by midnight on 31 October in the relevant year; if you miss this deadline you will need to file your return online. If you send in your tax return online it must reach HMRC by midnight on 31 January. So the 2012/13 paper return will need to be filed by 31 October 2013 and the 2012/13 online return will need to be filed by 31 January 2014.

You'll have to pay a £100 penalty if HMRC doesn't receive your tax return on time. The later you send your return after the 31 January, the more penalties you're likely to pay.

Sending your tax return online has many advantages. For example, your figures are calculated automatically and you'll know right away what you owe or what HMRC owes you, but to file online you need to sign up for HMRC Online Services first – so don't start to make your plans at the last minute, as you will need to receive passwords, etc., in the post before you can proceed.

5.2 Repairs and Renewals

If space permitted, I could write a whole book about repairs and renewals, or repairs and maintenance. It is the area of biggest confusion, and is one of the areas that HMRC get most excited about.

It is also the area that most accountants get hung up about: remember that they work for you not HMRC. We discussed, earlier, the need to have the *appropriate* professionals on your side – and this is an area where, sadly, so many accountants get it wrong.

You will recall the explanation of the difference between revenue and capital expenditure; with property, this is the area where you can leave a lot of money on HMRC's table.

At the risk of repeating things, if you can get an expense treated as revenue in the year it was spent, then you will reduce the taxable profit or, maybe, transform a profit into a loss.

Again don't underestimate the impact of inflation. A £5,000 expense included in your accounts *now* is worth far more than a £5,000 deduction when you come to sell.

So let's start with the fundamentals and then flesh out from there with some practical examples.

- When the property is first brought into rental market expenditure to make it available and fit for purpose is CAPITAL expenditure

- Restoring a property to its previous condition is REVENUE expenditure

- Enhancement expenditure will be CAPITAL expenditure.

We are always looking to treat repair expenditure as revenue; a simple step that will save you thousands of pounds is to delay the expenditure until after the property has been let for an initial period. This will save much potential debate and maybe even conflict with HMRC as to what is *revenue* and what is *capital*.

Needless to say the property has to be habitable, so if you buy a complete wreck this might be a tough strategy to follow – but there is no reason why you can't put people in on an assured shorthold tenancy (AST) for a short a period as desired. I'm reliably informed that an AST can be for as short a period as a week. How long you make yours, before the work starts, is a matter for your risk profile.

HMRC's view is that expenditure to rectify 'normal wear and tear' (which is, helpfully, undefined) would remain allowable. So if your property starts off as being fit for purpose and all it needs is a lick of paint and a deep clean, then such expenditure will be allowable as 'repairs'.

Tax Tip

Where there may be some debate with HMRC, arm yourself with, and have within the property file, pictures of the property on acquisition; notes as to why it was habitable; and pictures after.

Note that this strategy obviously would not work where a mortgage company imposed a retention because the property was uninhabitable; here, clearly, you would need to carry out your works in order to make the property suitable.

This is a tax-saving book rather than a tax manual but, for this section, please forgive the additional detail and examples: they will make your life easier in the long run.

The cost of *repairing* a worn or dilapidated asset is normally an allowable expense. *Replacing* the whole or the 'entirety' of an asset is not a repair – it is capital expenditure and thus not an allowable expense. What forms the asset or 'entirety' is a question of fact. You need to decide whether the asset is a separate asset or is part of a bigger asset.

Teague owns a number of residential properties that are let out. The properties are not furnished lettings. The boiler in one property needs replacing. As the new boiler has to be located in a different position, it is decided to modernise the kitchen as a whole. All the existing base units, wall units and sink etc. are stripped out and replaced, as is the fitted cooker and hob. New units of an equivalent quality are installed, but in a different layout to allow for the re-location of the boiler; finally, the kitchen is re-plastered and re-tiled. The entirety is the house, not the fitted kitchen. The new kitchen is slightly different, but it does the same job as before. Teague has simply replaced the old kitchen with a modern equivalent.

This is a repair and allowable expenditure.

The same principle would apply with the replacement of bathroom fittings.

Winterbottom runs a farm and has diversified so that he has six chalets that are used in a furnished holiday lettings business. One of the units is damaged beyond repair and Winterbottom replaces it with a new chalet of the same model. Most of the cost is covered by insurance, so Winterbottom only has to spend £2,500. The chalet is an identifiable asset in its own right. Winterbottom has replaced an asset and so the £2,500 is not an allowable expense.

For many years, Winterbottom has only carried out limited repairs to the drive from the road to his farmyard. In the spring, the dairy company tells him that the drive has deteriorated to the state that, unless it is repaired, their tankers will be unable to call at his farm. Reluctantly the drive is repaired. The tarmac was removed and the sub-surface repaired. The drive was then re-surfaced and new kerbing added as necessary, to bring the drive up to modern standards. As a result of the work, the drive was brought back to standard; there was no improvement involved. The drive is an asset in its own right; however it has not been replaced, merely surfaced so this is a repair.

Here's another

McBride has a garage in which he stores his van and building equipment. The garage is run down and needs major work. If McBride decides not to spend money on repairing the existing garage and has it knocked down and a new garage built, then that is not a repair, it is a replacement. It does not matter whether McBride chose to replace the asset, or was forced to, for instance because the building burnt down. The cost is capital expenditure and the whole cost is not an allowable expense. The fact that replacing the asset is the cheapest and most effective option does not make the expenditure allowable; it remains capital expenditure.

If, instead of simply repairing the asset, it is improved or upgraded, then all the cost of the work is not an allowable deduction for tax purposes. It is capital expenditure. Whether something has been repaired or improved is a question of fact.

So that you can decide whether or not the costs are allowable, you have to look at the nature and extent of the work carried out, but care needs to be taken where a complete programme of works has been carried out, as *some* works may simply be repairs, while others are alterations or improvements. With changes in regulations or technology it may not be practical or possible to carry out a repair using the same materials or equipment as originally used.

If the work amounts to an alteration or improvement then there is:

- No revenue deduction for any part of the expenditure. This includes things like redecoration after the main work has been done (although note that redecoration would *ordinarily* be a revenue expense)

- No revenue deduction for any notional expenditure for what it would have cost to simply repair the asset.

Gibson trades from premises that consist of a showroom and warehouse. Gibson decides to modernise the premises. Builders completely renew the roof, refurbish the staff kitchen, extend the showroom by demolishing an interior wall and building a new one and installing a new floor and false ceiling to modernise the extended showroom area.

The new roof simply returns the roof to its original condition. It is neither an alteration nor improvement; it is simply a repair of the building. In the same way, the refurbishment of the staff kitchen is simply a repair of the building. These are allowable expenses.

The work carried out on the storeroom/showroom has resulted in a larger showroom, to a higher standard. This is therefore an alteration and improvement. This is not an allowable expense.

Colclough runs a property business. One of the houses needs repairs to the roof. He takes the opportunity to convert the attic into an additional bedroom. Colclough has chosen not to simply repair the property, but has altered the property by converting unusable space into another room. The whole of the cost is disallowable. Were this simply a repair to the roof, then that would be a repair.

Technology and building practices change over time. When the time comes for an asset to be repaired, you may find that you have to use new technology – indeed, your builders may be legally required to do so. So when the work is done it's important in deciding whether changes in technology have led to an improvement. As technology changes over time, something that would be accepted as an improvement in year one may, by year five, be simply a repair for tax purposes. This is because that technology is no longer seen as an improvement and is simply what is used for the job – the industry standard for that type of work. Using that technology does not change the character of the building.

One example of this is double glazing. At one time, replacing single-glazed windows with double glazing was an improvement. Over time, double glazing became the industry norm, and this meant that replacing single glazing with double glazing ceased to be an improvement (and thus capital expenditure) but became allowable expenditure for tax purposes as it was simply replacing like with *available* like.

Jeffrey has a property business and is advised that the boiler in one property needs to be replaced. Jeffrey is told that he cannot simply replace the boiler with one of the same type because, since 1st April 2007, it has been a legal requirement (in England and Wales) that all gas boilers installed must be a condensing model. In addition, the old boiler was rated in Imperial units and boilers are now measured in the equivalent metric unit. Jeffrey chooses to replace the boiler with a condensing boiler that is the closest equivalent in capability. The new boiler is smaller and has to be installed on a different wall, so that it can condense outside. Jeffrey takes the opportunity to install additional kitchen units as tenants have commented about the lack of storage space. Although the tank is slightly larger, the reality is that Jeffrey has simply used the modern equivalent of the original tank. The result is that the cost of the boiler is still revenue expenditure. However, the cost of the additional kitchen units is an improvement and not an allowable expense – even though it was carried out at the same time.

If the asset is altered or improved then it is capital expenditure; it is not allowable expenditure. In some cases, if the asset had not been altered or improved, then the business would still have had to have the asset repaired. The cost of these repairs would have been allowable.

The business does not get relief for the repairs it would have had to pay for, i.e. for the 'notional repairs'. This is because the business did not have the asset repaired and the treatment for tax purposes follows what actually happened, not what might have happened. As the business chose to have the asset altered or improved, it is capital expenditure, and thus not an allowable expense.

Dawes recognises that the office roof needs repairing. Rather than simply carrying out the repairs, it is decided to have the roof space opened up and additional windows put in, so it can be used as office space. Dawes cannot claim the cost of the roof repairs, as they did not take place. Instead he chose to have additional work done. This is an improvement and is thus capital expenditure. Dawes cannot claim the cost that would have been incurred because it ended up being an improvement not a repair.

A repair which restores a worn or dilapidated asset is normally an allowable expense. It is quite likely that the asset may need to be repaired and that these repairs do not arise from use in the current business. Things to consider:

- Repairs carried out just after they acquired the asset does not, of itself, mean that the cost of the repair is disallowable

- The fact that the repairs were needed when the asset was acquired does not, of itself, mean that the cost of the repair is disallowable

- The cost of the repair will be a capital expense *if it is effectively part of the cost of acquiring the asset*. Whether the cost of the repairs is part of the cost of the asset is a question of fact.

So what makes a repair *part of the cost of acquiring the asset*? This can be answered by asking another question: what was the condition of the asset? Was it in working order, or was it an asset that needed repairing to enable it to be used in the business.

Pointers to the expense being a *repair* and allowable as a deduction include:

- The repairs are part of the routine normal maintenance cycles,

- The price paid was not affected by the condition of the asset,

- The price was adjusted, but only to reflect where the asset was in the routine maintenance cycle

- The asset could be used in the longer term in the business without being repaired.

Pointers to the expense *being part of the cost of acquiring the asset* and thus not allowable as a deduction include:

- The asset could not be used in the business without being repaired,

- The asset could only be used in the short term and its long-term use was dependent upon the repairs being carried out,

- The purchase price of the asset reflected the fact that the asset needed repairing to be useable.

Moore buys an empty property for an existing property business. The price reflects the fact that thieves have stripped the house of copper fittings. Moore has new plumbing installed. In addition, Moore decides the exterior needs re-painting. Moore cannot claim for the cost of the new plumbing and related plastering and decorating, as the house could not be used until this work was done and the price reflected the condition. In effect, it was a cost of acquiring a house and putting it into a condition that it could be let.

Moore can claim for the painting of the exterior. This is a job that has to be done every few years. It is normal maintenance work. Moore can claim this as an expense even though the work was done just after the asset was acquired.

If thieves hadn't made the place uninhabitable and it could have been occupied in its present condition, then those costs would all have been treated as revenue not capital.

Finally in this section on repairs, especially where a lot of repair work has been done, is to consider whether the 'character of the asset' has changed as a result of the work. Put simply, you need to ask whether it is the same object before and after the work. If, after the work, it simply does the same job as before, then this pointer suggests that the work is a repair.

Richards owns a Victorian building that has been divided into student flats. The electrician recommends that the building needs re-wiring. Richards decides to take the opportunity and have the building modernised.

The whole house is rewired, the heating system is partially replaced, the kitchens in all flats are replaced, together with two of the bathrooms. Three windows are replaced and the property redecorated inside and out.

As a result of the work, Richards still has a property divided into the same number of student flats, capable of providing the same standard of accommodation for the same number of students. Looked at as a whole, the character of the asset has not changed as a result of the work. There may be small items of alterations, but the overall programme is simply a repair. It is important to recognise that a considerable amount of work can be carried out without changing the character of the asset.

Richards has another property let as student flats, which lies in an area that is now attracting investment. So rather than refurbishing the property as student accommodation, Richards has the same work carried out to a much higher standard and converts the building into flats suitable for long-term letting to people in a high income bracket. Looked at as a whole, the character of the asset has changed, from short-let student accommodation to up-market long-term lettings; thus the expenditure would be deemed to be capital not revenue.

So for those of you knocking single lets into multi-lets – this applies to you!

However, just to confuse matters, look at this example:

For many years Ackford has owned retail premises in an historic town centre. A survey reveals that the property is in an extremely poor state of repair. He decides that the premises should be gutted and modernised. The work carried out, as set out in the invoices, includes:

- *The roof was stripped, all rotten roof timbers removed, the roof replaced in the same position and with the same outline so there is no additional space*

- *Corrugated asbestos roofing installed in the sixties was replaced by tiles*

- *The first floor was stripped out and reinstalled, supported on steel joists rather than timber*

- *On the ground floor, oak flooring was stripped out and replaced by a concrete floor that provided a flat, even surface*

- *The shop front was replaced*

- *The oak beam over the shop was replaced by a steel joist*

- *The oak pillar supporting the front corner of the building was replaced by a steel stanchion*

- *Any visible steelwork was clad in salvaged oak to maintain the appearance of the property*

- *The electrical system was renewed.*

The aim of the work is to maintain the appearance of the store. There is no change to the size of the sales area. The question to ask is whether, looked at in the round, the work resulted in a restoration of what was there before – or did it create something new?

In this case, the property may have been 'gutted and modernised' but the character of the asset remained unchanged. Looked at from the point of view of how the building was used, the work was simply a restoration to enable it to be used to do the job it had long been used for. So all that expenditure would be classed as repairs!

Tax Tip

The above examples have, hopefully, demonstrated how repairs can be a complete minefield and, yes, may lead to some debate with HMRC.

Arm yourself, and have within the property file, pictures of the property on acquisition; notes as to why it was or wasn't habitable; clear and unambiguous invoices from tradesman – especially where these are big projects – and, yes, pictures after.

Finally, if you brain is not fried enough – don't forget that you can bring *provisions* into your accounts. Provisions are not stuff you get before you go off to Scout camp – but an accounting term, whereby we can bring in the cost even though we've not yet paid for it.

In an example above, Colclough needed a new roof but chose instead to add another bedroom, thus turning all the revenue expense into a capital expense. You will recall that had he simply replaced the roof then it would have been a repair. So here, let's just repair the roof. It is early March and Colclough is keen to get the repair cost into 2012/13 accounts for the tax relief but his roofer can't start work until May. No worries; Colclough gets an estimate and a contract signed with his roofer for the work to be undertaken in May – and Colclough can now bring this cost into his accounts as a provision.

Colclough reduces his 2012/13 tax bill and thus the amount he has to pay on 31 January.

Tax Tip

Where expenses are on the horizon, get a contact in place before the year end to bring forward the tax relief.

5.3 Landlord's Energy Saving Allowance (LESA)

The Landlord's Energy Saving Allowance was introduced to encourage landlords to improve the energy efficiency of let residential properties. It is an allowance for the cost of acquiring and installing certain energy-saving items where this kind of expenditure cannot normally be deducted when calculating taxable profits and is not eligible for capital allowances.

The allowance is available on qualifying expenditure on specified energy saving items incurred before 6 April 2015. LESA can be claimed on the following energy-saving items in let residential property, provided the expenditure is incurred on or after the dates specified below, and before 6 April 2015:

- Loft insulation   From 6 April 2004

- Cavity wall insulation   From 6 April 2004

- Solid wall insulation   From 7 April 2005

- Draught proofing   From 6 April 2006

- Hot water system insulation From 6 April 2006

- Floor insulation   From 6 April 2007.

The maximum (total) allowance is £1,500 per dwelling house, which means that, where a single building contains two or more dwellings, the landlord can claim up to £1,500 *on each dwelling*.

Expenditure may need to be apportioned, for example where a landlord installs energy- saving items in:

- A building that only partly comprises let residential property

- A building containing more than one dwelling house

- A property that is let by more than one landlord.

In these circumstances a just and reasonable apportionment of the expenditure must be made between all the properties which benefit from the energy-saving item. A landlord should only claim for the expenditure which benefits the residential property that they let, reduced to £1,500 for each dwelling-house if necessary.

A landlord cannot claim the allowance:

- If they are claiming rent-a-room relief in respect of the dwelling house

- If the property business includes the commercial letting of furnished holiday accommodation

- If the expenditure is incurred in respect of energy-saving items in a dwelling house which, at the time when the items are installed:
    - Is in the course of construction, or
    - Is comprised in land in which the person claiming the deduction under this section does not have an interest or is in the course of acquiring an interest or further interest.

Tax Tip

Make sure that you claim your Energy Saving Allowance

5.4 Furnished lettings

The difference between 'rental income' and 'furnished rental income' is, spookily, the word 'furnished'! So what is a furnished property?

Well, HMRC tells us:

> *"A furnished property is one that is capable of normal occupation without the tenant having to provide their own beds, chairs, tables, sofas and other furnishings, cooker etc. The provision of nominal furnishings will not meet this requirement."*

Helpfully, though, they then fail to tell us what their definition of 'nominal furnishings' is, so in the absence of that insight I would suggest that – as long as they have somewhere to eat, somewhere to relax somewhere to sleep and a reasonable carpet under their feet – then they have a furnished property. It may not be to your particular taste but, hey, this is a box to make us money.

No initial allowance will be given for the capital costs incurred when you furnish the property at the outset, but thereafter HMRC will allow a deduction for the fact that your property is furnished.

The deduction is given in one of two ways:

- Replacement cost of goods – but not initial cost *or*

- A wear and tear allowance.

You, the owner, can choose which way you decide to go – but once on that path there is no way off, so think carefully before deciding which route to follow. You can't decide on a property-to-property basis.

Tax Tip

You don't have to decide in advance which way to claim so weigh up all the costs in year one and then decide.

You can, however, go one route for properties in your name and one route for properties in the name of your spouse or for properties in joint names.

Replacement

There will be no tax relief for the initial cost but thereafter if an item is replaced or renewed then the cost of that replacement will be written off in full. So as items are replaced then claim as an expense.

Tax Tip

It may be worth initially furnishing with cheaper furniture bought off ebay or at local charity shops and then replacing with newer modern stuff and claiming the 100% deduction.

Weir started with a perfectly good leather sofa that cost £100 on ebay. Within a year, it was replaced with a new one which cost £1,000 – so Weir claimed the full deduction of £1,000.

Wear and tear allowance

Here you can claim a deduction of 10% of the net rental income against your rental income; net rental income being the annual rent less any contributions that you make. So, say you paid the water rates, then this cost will be deducted.

Typically this is the better way as:

- The tax relief is immediate

- It is given in perpetuity: each year you will claim the 10% deduction

- Furniture lasts forever these days.

Depending on your risk profile you can achieve the 10% wear and tear allowance for very little outlay and being diligent with your paperwork. For a £250 net outlay you get along to Argos or other suitable outlets and you purchase an inflatable bed, two inflatable chairs, a foldaway set of tables and chairs and some crockery and cutlery and a basic set of pots and pans. Inflate as appropriate and cover with suitable drapes; put rest of furniture in place: you now have a furnished letting where people can eat, people can relax and people can sleep. Having dressed the property you advertise the property on a furnished assured shorthold tenancy (AST).

Some tenants may accept your generous 'furniture pack'; others may decline. If they decline, simply note this fact on the AST, ask them to confirm this in writing and you can now legitimately claim the 10% wear and tear allowance.

Millican has a furnished rental property:

- *Annual rental income: £10,000*

- *10% wear and tear allowance: £1,000*

- *Net saving, year 1: £750 (1,000-250)*

- *Total allowances over next nine years: £9,000*

- *Paperwork all sorted*

- *Deflate and move to attic if they decline.*

5.5 Furnished Holiday Lettings

As well as single lets or houses of multiple occupancy (HMOs) some of you may venture into the furnished holiday lettings market. Done well, the yields can be significantly higher than single lets, though naturally a bit more work is involved on a weekly basis.

If you have furnished holiday lettings, either in the UK or the EEA (European Economic Area), you will need to complete the relevant section of the self-assessment return. The special rules for furnished holiday lettings changed in 2011/12 – and not necessarily for the better!

Profit from properties that meet the qualifying tests for furnished holiday lettings is taxed following the normal rental business (i.e. property income) calculation rules. The qualifying tests are as follows – and you will need to satisfy all three of the following tests if a letting is to qualify:

1. The *availability* condition: during the period the accommodation is *available* for commercial letting as holiday accommodation to the public for *at least 210* days

2. The *letting condition*: during the period, the accommodation *is commercially let* as holiday accommodation to the public *for at least 105 days*

3. The *pattern of occupation* condition: basically, the accommodation must not be let for periods of longer-term occupation for more than 155 days during the year.

Conditions 1 and 3 are fairly easy to hit, but 2 may present a few problems.

Tax Tip

Unless you bought an existing holiday cottage it will take time for the lettings to build, so market the property as early as you can and as aggressively as you can and you will easily get to 105 days: after all that's only 15 weeks a year.

The good news is that furnished holiday lettings are treated as trades for some tax purposes and therefore have some great tax advantages over other lettings. The advantages under the special rules are:

1. Entitlement to plant and machinery capital allowances on furniture, furnishings, white goods etc. in the let property, as well as on plant and machinery used outside the property (such as vans and tools). Note that the 10% wear and tear allowance that you would be entitled to if you have an ordinary rental business is not available as an alternative. There are no capital allowances for the cost of the property itself or the land on which it stands

2. Capital Gains Tax reliefs for traders such as Business Asset Rollover Relief, Entrepreneurs' Relief, relief for gifts of business assets and relief for loans to traders, are all available here

3. Profits count as earnings for pension purposes.

You will need to work out the profit or loss from these furnished holiday lettings separately from any other rental business, to make sure that the special advantages are restricted to the furnished holiday lettings that meet the qualifying tests.

To qualify as a furnished holiday letting the accommodation must be in the UK or EEA and commercially let. The EEA comprises the 27 states in the European Union (EU) plus Iceland, Liechtenstein and Norway. Letting outside the EEA does not qualify.

'Commercial' means let on a commercial basis and with a view to making a profit, which seems fair enough. Close season lettings will be unlikely to produce a profit but normally help towards the cost of maintaining the property. This letting can still be treated as commercial. On the other hand, lettings to friends or relatives at zero or nominal rents, whilst very generous, would not be considered commercial.

Tax Tip

If you do let to friends and family, charge them the full commercial rent –
but, being a generous host, furnish them with a super welcome
pack of goodies.

Accommodation is 'furnished' if the visitor is entitled to the use of furniture; needless to say, there should be sufficient furniture provided for normal occupation.

Properties in EEA countries other than the UK qualify as furnished holiday lettings, but note that all the properties you own in the UK are taxed as one furnished holiday lettings business – and all the properties you own in other EEA states are taxed as a separate business. You will therefore need to keep separate records for each business.

Because of tax advantages that furnished holiday lettings get, you will need to work out the furnished holiday lettings profit or loss separately from any other rental business.

Where furnished holiday lettings satisfy the qualifying tests, this does not provide any automatic qualification for Inheritance Tax Business Property Relief, though there's every reason that it should.

A supply of holiday accommodation by a registered VAT trader will generally carry VAT at the standard rate, whether or not it is holiday accommodation that meets the qualifying furnished holiday lettings tests, but this may not be the case for off-season letting. Since the profit is taxable as rental income, no Class 4 NIC nor Class 2 will be payable.

Note that all of the furnished holiday lettings properties that you let on your own are treated as one business. If you are in partnership all the properties you let in the same partnership, are treated as one business.

You can't amalgamate the properties you own *individually* with any you own *in partnership*.

If you are lucky enough to have an EEA furnished holiday lettings business in more than one country, then all the properties in non-UK states form one business. You can't amalgamate a UK and an EEA set of properties.

Where a property is kept solely for letting as furnished holiday accommodation, but is in fact closed for part of the year because there are no customers, you can deduct the whole of expenses such as insurance, interest, etc., provided there is no private use.

Tax Tip

However tempting to use a holiday let for your own personal use be mindful of the rules regarding availability and the need for the lettings to be commercial.

If you are ever holidaying in the United Kingdom, then you will be more than welcome here at any time of the year:

www.northumbrian-cottages.info/northumberland-coast/craster-embleton-area/lilac-cottage-dunstan

You will see that we use a consolidator for leverage. In other words we have people to take the bookings, collect the money and change the sheets so that we can do other things. Sure they charge a fee but you can't do everything.

5.6 Rent-a-room Relief

To generate some additional income you may choose to let out a room to a lodger in your home. If you do, then you can claim rent-a-room relief whereby you can earn £4,250 tax free. Yes, that's tax free.

Note that it must be your home and not a property that you are currently letting from a landlord.

You will provide the lodger with a furnished room and shared use of all common rooms and, maybe, make an additional charge for meals cleaning or laundry. So long as this is below £4,250, you have no tax to pay.

Tax Tip

If, after deducting expenses, you have a loss then that loss can be offset against other rental income, assuming that you have some. The trick here is not to go the rent-a-room relief route but combine with all your property income on the tax return.

If the rental income exceeds £4,250 then you will be taxed on rental income less expenses. You now have the choice to take advantage of another tax tip.

Tax Tip

Instead of paying tax on income less expenses, go for income less the rent-a-room tax free allowance.

Robinson lets two rooms out for £50 per week or £5,200 per year. Robinson has expenses of £1,500, so shows a taxable profit of £3,700. However if Robinson elects to be taxed on rental over £4,250 then Robinson will only pay tax on £950 (£5,200- £4,250).

That could also work the other way. Bowe lets two rooms at £80 per week or £8,320 per annum. After expenses of £4,800, Bowe has a taxable profit of £3,520; if he had elected for the rent-a-room scheme, however, his taxable profit would have been around £500 more: £4,070 (£8,320- £4,250).

Tax Tip

It is at the taxpayer's discretion whether or not they claim rent-a-room relief – so long as the election is made within 12 months after 31 January following the tax year; so for 2012/13, the election would need to be made by 31 January 2015.

5.7 Rental Losses

While we are all investing in property to make a profit, in the initial years there may be losses; if we hit some major repairs the chances are the property itself may turn in a loss.

Depending on how or where the losses arose they will be subject to different treatment.

Losses arising from UK property rental income in any year are first set off against other profits from rental income in that year. To the extent that they are unused, they are carried forward in perpetuity – and in some cases may go with you to the grave.

It goes without saying that if you cease to own rental property then you will lose the losses. So if you think that you may restart in the future but, for now, want to liquidate your portfolio, maybe keep at least one so that you continue to have property rental income and thus preserve the losses.

Note that losses cannot be transferred to your spouse.

While we have been looking all the time to maximise expenditure, particularly over the treatment of repairs, it may be that, where we have large losses, we are less aggressive with the claims – and thereby creating profits to absorb the losses.

Losses from furnished holiday lettings have their own special rules and losses arising may now only be carried forward to future profits. Prior to 2010/11 these losses could have been used against other income from the same tax year! Never mind.

Losses from overseas properties will be covered when we look at the treatment of overseas property income.

5.8 Taxation

Clearly everyone invests in property to make a profit and generate cashflow, though given all the expenses that we can offset, particularly in the first year, it will be unlikely that there will be a profit in year one. That loss will be carried forward to offset against future profits and once those losses have been exhausted it's time to pay the taxman.

Before the taxman has his chunk, your personal allowance should be deducted and then tax will be applied at the appropriate rate.

The amount you can earn tax-free (your personal allowance) changes each year, as do the rates of tax. Any profit will be taxed at your marginal rate of tax. You can find the current rates and allowances here:

http://www.hmrc.gov.uk/rates/

If (2013/14) you are in employment and a basic rate taxpayer, you will pay tax at 20%; if you are a higher rate tax payer you'll pay an element at 40%; or, if an additional rate taxpayer, you'll pay at 45%. As mentioned elsewhere, if you own property jointly, and one partner is a higher rate taxpayer and the other a basic rate taxpayer, then it may be worth more of the ownership and income going to them.

Mr & Mrs Pullen have a portfolio generating £15,000 net profit per year. Mrs Pullen is a higher rate tax payer and Mr Pullen a basic rate taxpayer so, at the outset, they allocated ownership and income 90/10.

A simple 50/50 split would have generated a total tax bill of £4,875, but with their 90/10 allocation the tax bill is £3,375 – so they have saved £1,500. The savings would be even greater if Pullen did not work.

Your tax liability due under self -assessment, which will include all income, is paid in three chunks:

- In the year of assessment, a payment on account on 31 January. For 2012/13 that will be 31 January 2013

- In the year of assessment a payment on account on 31 July following the year of assessment, so for 2012/13 that will be 31 July 2013

- A balancing payment on 31 January following the year of assessment, so for 2012/13 that will be 31 January 2014.

In the first year that you self-assess there will be no payments on account and the full chunk will be due 31 January. Thereafter, you will be paying a chunk of tax every six months with the payments on account being 50% of the previous year's total tax liability.

This cycle will be broken however if:

- The payment on account is less than £1,000

- The payment on account is less than 20% of the total tax liability

- Your return generates a refund.

Tax is a consequence of running a profitable business and it's essential to put away some tax in a moneybox ready for the day that the taxman comes knocking on your door.

The Richest Man in Babylon is a book by George Samuel Clason which dispenses financial advice through a collection of parables set in ancient Babylon. I'm a great fan of this book, and if you've not read it, treat yourself. It's a quick easy read – and you now know that it is tax deductible! In the book Clason advocates saving a percentage of everything you earn to a tax pot (typically 20%). There are other pots (I won't spoil the read) but it's very powerful and amazing how the tax pot grows. Then when the tax man comes calling you have the money in your tax pot and it may well be that you have put away more than you needed to – in which case another pot can be topped up.

Tax filing deadlines were mentioned earlier, but there is also another date that is worth remembering, if you are in employment, and that is 30 December. For 2012/13 that will be 30 December 2013 and, if you meet this deadline online or paper return by 31 October and provided the tax is below a certain level (currently £3,000) then HMRC will collect the tax the following year through your PAYE Code.

What that means is that you will effectively get an interest-free loan to clear your tax debt over the next 12 months. Yes, you will need to tick box 3 on page TR5 on the return – but it will certainly ease cashflow.

To protect you from paying unreasonable tax deductions and thus having nothing to live on, you won't be able to pay the tax you owe through your tax code in the following circumstances:

- You don't have enough PAYE income to enable HMRC to collect it

- You would pay more than 50 per cent of your PAYE income in tax

- You would end up paying more than twice as much tax as you normally do each time you receive your pay or pension.

Beaumont's completed 2012/13 self-assessment return was filed online by 30 November 2013. He had a tax liability of £1,320. As he had ticked box 3 on page TR5, his tax was collected in 12 equal chunks in 2014/15. So £110 would be collected each month. So although his net monthly pay would be reduced, Beaumont did not have to write a cheque for £1,320 just after Christmas – when cashflow is almost always at its tightest.

5.9 Other Taxes

As a property investor you will not pay Class 2 nor Class 4 National Insurance, which is a profit-based tax.

CHAPTER 6

Avoiding Taxes in a Property Trading Business

6.1 Introduction

As we saw in Chapter Four, many of the deductions that apply to a property investment business will also apply to a property trading business.

Where you are trading in property then you will be taxed under a completely different set of rules to those that would apply to a property investment business.

Equally you will have a trading business for your deal packaging service, letting agency or whoever you choose to earn money from property, so it will do no harm to flag up some important differences

The main areas where a trading business differs from an investment business are as follows:

- Properties bought for development are treated as *stock* rather than *assets* held as investments

- You can choose your own year end and thus the date to which you prepare accounts

- You will pay tax on the profits you make when you sell a property

- You can trade as a limited company, sole trader, partnership or limited liability partnership; each will be taxed differently

- Sole traders and partnerships will pay income tax, Class 2 and Class 4 National Insurance, while limited companies corporation tax and limited liability partnerships however they have been set up

- Traders get cut more slack in terms of deductions, particularly where things don't proceed

- Capital allowances will only be claimed on their own assets, not properties held in trading stock

- Trading losses receive a more forgiving treatment.

6.2 Trading Stock

As a property *trader* you are simply buying properties to add value – whether that be from a complete refurbishment or by adding further rooms, title split or whatever.

So, rather like a shop that buys in stock to sell, your business is exactly the same. All of the costs in acquiring this property are part of your 'cost of sales'. It will not, and will never, be an investment: you plan to sell on as quickly as possible and make a tidy profit.

Of even better news is that we can avoid the heated debate as to whether the expenses are of a revenue or capital nature, because here they are all revenue related. So, for example, whereas an *investor* has to carry forward the cost of the legal fees, here, as a *trader*, they are part of the cost of the property. Where an investor has to carry forward the cost of adding a new room in the roof, here it will be a cost of sale.

One would hope that project gets turned around during the year and doesn't appear in stock at the year end – but not every project goes according to plan. And if the property remains unsold then the expenses incurred are not yet written off but instead taken into stock.

O'Gara buys a property for £120,000 and incurs additional costs in securing the property of £5,000. Work commences immediately, but the weather conspires against O'Gara and the builders such that, by the December year end, the project has not been completed. At that date the build costs amount to £15,000. In the accounts (but shown as stock not an expense) will be the cost of expenditure to date, namely £140,000.

Despite continued wind and rain the project is completed after further build costs of £25,000.

When the accounts now come to be prepared they will show in cost of sales (i.e. a revenue expense) £165,000 (i.e. the total cost of obtaining the property and making it ready for re-sale) which will be deducted from the sales proceeds.

Techie Point: typically, as with O'Gara, stock is valued at the *lower* of cost and 'net realisable value'. So with O'Gara that would be £140,000. But let's suppose it was a much bigger project; the whole property took much longer to renovate or add value to, and the market value actually went down. In these circumstances we would need to show this, in the accounts, at the lower net realisable value.

Just to add further confusion if a contract was in place for the sale of the property, accountants would get very excited about apportioning the overall value of the contract. Be aware of it but leave it for them to get excited about.

6.3 Choose your Year End

While investors have to run accounts to 5 April, no such rules apply to property traders, be they sole traders partnerships, limited companies or limited liability partnerships.

Some will choose December, so that the business runs to the calendar year; owners can then relax at Christmas, knowing that their work is done and prepare the ship for its next journey. Others simply choose the month in which they formed the company.

Whatever the year end, it offers an excellent opportunity for tax planning. While, for an investor, it's hard to shift rental income it's much easier for a trader – and can gain significant cashflow advantages.

Bennett Limited makes accounts up to 30 June. A property has been developed and is ready to sell and a buyer has been found. The lawyers are progressing well and discussion moves to an exchange date. "30 June," suggests the purchaser – but Bennett suggests 1 July. Why?

Well, on this deal Bennett will make £100,000 profit and – ignoring everything else within the company for this example – will pay £20,000 in corporation tax. This will be due nine months after the year end.

If they exchange contracts on 30 June 2013, this sale will fall into the accounts to 30 June 2013, with the tax due on 1 April 2014.

If they exchange on 1 July 2013, this will fall into the accounts to 30 June 2014 with the tax due on 1 April 2015. So by delaying completion by one day Bennett has secured a further 12 months to pay corporation tax and has £20,000 additional working capital.

If Bennett were a sole trader the profits would have been assessed in 2013/14, with tax payable 31 January 2015 – or with the July exchange assessed in 2014/15 with tax due 31 January 2016. Again, a twelve-

month cashflow advantage. (The complexities of payments on account have been ignored for this example.)

Tax Tip

Use the year end to your advantage to bring forward expenditure or defer income.

6.4 Taxation

Depending on which vehicle you use to trade, you will pay tax on your profits – so let's look briefly at each form of business.

Sole trader

A sole trader will pay income tax on his profits via self-assessment and, in addition, Class 4 National Insurance (which has nothing to do with National Insurance and is simply a profits-based tax) plus Class 2 National Insurance, which is a nominal amount. Current rates are available here:

http://www.hmrc.gov.uk/rates/

Note that if you have self-employment alongside paid employment you may be able to apply for a refund or deferment as strangely HMRC limit the amount of National Insurance that you have to pay.

Partnership

A partnership is two or more people working in business for profit and is usually the next step up from a sole trader. The partners will pay tax on their share of the profit – not drawings. Edwards & John are in equal partnership and make profits of £100,000. Being prudent they only draw £24,000 a year from the business. Regardless of that they will pay tax on their share of profit £50,000 for the year. As with a sole trader, they will need to self-assess and pay income tax, Class 4 and Class 2 National Insurance contributions.

As well as submitting their own individual returns, the partnership as a separate entity must file a self-assessment return.

A partnership has 'joint and several liability'. What that means in practice is that any one partner can engage in a contract that is enforceable against both parties.

Edwards buys himself, using hire purchase, a new state-of-the-art JCB without telling John his business partner. The partnership falls into hard times but the debt to the HP Company still exists and they can pursue any other partner for the debt.

Limited Liability Partnership (LLP)

The best of both worlds? Well, possibly in that the problem referred to above regarding unlimited liability will not raise its ugly head and there will be more onerous reporting at Companies House.

The partners in a Limited Liability Partnership can be other limited companies or sole traders or indeed partnerships with profits distributed according to the Limited Liability Partnership Agreement and taxed accordingly.

Underwood Properties LLP is owned 80% by Underwood Ltd and 20% by Underwood. Underwood Limited will pay corporation tax on its share of the profit and Underwood income tax on his share.

Complicated, confusing – and sometimes a sledgehammer to crack a nut – but this form of business may sometimes be useful in tax planning (and that in itself could be a book) so please seek further professional advice.

Limited company

A company will pay corporation tax on its profits. There is also more onerous reporting at Companies House, and your annual accounts are public documents – so competitors are able to access elements of your trading history and profitability. Current rates of corporation tax can be found here:

http://www.hmrc.gov.uk/rates/corp.htm

Whichever of the trading vehicles is used, none will benefit from the Annual Exemption for Capital Gains Tax that individual property investors benefit from.

Tax Tip

Spend some time at the outset to get the right business structure in place and, thus, pay the least amount of tax.

6.5 Forgiving Expense Regime

In Chapter Four we looked at common expenses to both property investors and traders and flagged up where, sometimes, the dice rolls in the trader's favour.

6.6 Capital Allowances

The basic rules have not changed simply because we are now a trader, and can be revisited in Chapter Four.

Traders, though, are more likely to have more items of capital expenditure such as equipment and tools, and maybe vehicles (as well as computers and office equipment, that will be common to both types of business) on which they can claim allowances.

Remember that a trader will not claim any capital allowances on capital expenditure within a building project – all the costs will be treated as revenue expenditure and included in the annual profit and loss statement.

An investor, on the other hand, will have to treat such expenditure as capital – and thus be looking for items within the fabric of the building on which allowances can be claimed.

6.7 Losses

If an investor makes a loss then that has to be carried forward until a profit is made.

Depending on which trading vehicle you use, trading losses however can be offset against all of your other income and capital gains for the current year – and even the previous one! So if you've taken a real hit in the trading business some useful tax breaks can arise.

6.8 Corporation Tax and the Incorporation Debate

The million dollar question that I get asked the most is "Should I trade through a limited company?" And the million dollar answer that I always give is – "It depends!"

And the reason that, every time, I can confidently say "it depends" is that it genuinely does! In fact it depends so much that I could probably write another book on the whole subject.

Whether you choose to trade through a company depends on a variety of factors and there is thankfully no "one size fits all" solution. So let's deal with the key issues to address:

- Type and level of property income

- Your other sources of income

- Who are you buying for

- How long are you planning to be in business for.

There are many ways that people generate income from property, but the most typical will be:

- Buy & flip, in which case you are a property trader

- Buy & hold, in which case you are a property investor

- Deal packaging

- Lease options

- Rent to rent

- Creating low-end or high-end HMOs

- Lettings or estate agency.

Dealing with the first two, it's fair to say that a trading through a limited company provides a better result (from a tax perspective) for *income* – but holding property in your own name or joint names will produce a better result where there is *capital growth*. Not every time, but it's a safe generalisation.

For the purpose of this section I'm going to look at those top two (trader or investor) and, from that, you should be able to deduce which way is right for you for the other income streams.

If you are developing and flipping properties then you should be generating profits – and in certain cases, substantial profits. Any profit generated will be taxed at your marginal rate of tax.

In 2013/14 the basic rate of tax is 20%, a higher rate of 40% tax kicks in at £32,010 and additional rate tax of 45% at £150,000; current rates of income tax can be found here:

http://www.hmrc.gov.uk/incometax/basics.htm#6

Successful builders/developers will not want to be losing that amount of tax at the higher end of the scale, in which case it may be that these profits need to be sheltered within a limited company, where you will only pay corporation tax at 20%.

So, yes, a limited company may reduce the initial tax on the profit – but how will you extract the profit from the company? Essentially there are two ways to extract the profits: pay yourself a *salary* or take a post-tax *dividend*.

Salaries will attract Class 1 National Insurance, and the company will also have to pay National Insurance to pay you! That, in itself, makes salaries a very expensive way to extract profit, though of course the expense involved will be reduce the profit chargeable to corporation tax.

Alternatively, a dividend can be paid from post-tax profits; if you are a basic rate tax payer then no further tax will become payable because the dividend is treated as being paid net of basic rate tax with a credit for this being given in your tax computation. If you are a higher rate tax payer then you will pay additional tax through your self-assessment return.

In 2013/14, with a personal allowance of £9,440 and higher rate tax not kicking in until £32,010 you could pay yourself a tax-free dividend of

£41,450 if you have no other income. You could also pay your spouse or business partner a similar amount and, (of course, provided there are sufficient retained profits in the company) straddle the tax year-end and get double bubble, as shown in the second example below.

Gibbs Limited makes a profit of £125,000 and, after tax at 20% has a post-tax profit of £100,000 in the year to 31 December 2013. It decides to pay its shareholders (Mr & Mrs Gibbs) a dividend of £41,450 each on 31 March 2014. The dividend is paid with no further tax to pay. So the company has earned £125,000 and £82,900 (2 × £41450) has found its way to the shareholders, tax free. Who'd like some of that?

Another example with even better news.

Kiernan Limited makes a profit of £250,000 and, after tax at 20%, has a post-tax profit of £200,000 in the year to 30 April 2013. During the tax year 2012/13, interim dividends of £42,475 were paid to its shareholders, Mr and Mrs Kiernan, on 31 March 2013. A further dividend of £41,450 was paid to each on 7 April 2013 in the tax year 2013/14. The company has earned £250,000 and £167,850 has found its way to the shareholders, tax free, in the space of seven days!

Tax Tip

Pay yourself dividends to avoid the National Insurance cost and pay just before and just after the tax year-end for maximum cash in the shortest time.

Yes, you have to earn the profit in the first place – but see how cleverly you can legally avoid tax on those profits by using a limited company.

Incidentally, notice the stealth tax being applied! £42,475 was the amount you could earn at the lower rate, plus the personal allowance, in 2012/13; it dropped to £41,450 in 2013/14. A further £410 has mysteriously found its way out of your pocket to HMRC!

Another consideration is that as *employees* of the company you will pay tax and the company employing you will pay National Insurance on any benefits in kind. So, for example, if you buy a car through the company then you will be assessed on a 'benefit in kind'. Alternatively, you could go the mileage route and buy the car personally.

Capital Gains Tax (CGT) will be dealt with in another chapter, but a company does not benefit from the annual Capital Gains Tax allowance, so when it comes to sell an investment property it will pay more tax – as can be seen by this example.

Morgan Limited sells an investment property and makes a profit of £50,000 (for this example ignore any other reliefs). Morgan Limited will pay corporation tax at 20% (£10,000) leaving a net £40,000.

Mr & Mrs Morgan make a profit on their investment property of £50,000, which they sold in March 2013 i.e. in the tax year 2012/13. From this will be deducted the annual exemption of £10,600 each. As they are basic rate taxpayers, they will pay Capital Gains Tax of £5,184 which means that they are £4,816 better off than the directors of Morgan Limited.

There is also far more onerous reporting required for a limited company in that you will need to file accounts at Companies House.

If you are buying to hold, do you really want the capital growth of properties locked into a limited company – and the possibility of double taxation on your profits? If you are buying to hold and watch as the rent comes in, and the capital growth accrues then – as indicated earlier – you will probably want to buy in your own name or joint names.

But what if you are both higher rate tax payers? Do you really want to lose 45% of that income? Maybe, in *this* instance, it would be more sensible to earn the profits in a company and leave the post -tax profit to reinvest in more properties.

It's likely that as higher rate tax payers you are building a portfolio for later in life and will not be relying on the rental income at this stage.

Rates of Tax and Marginal Rates

Who are you buying these properties and creating this wealth for? Are you building a business that you can pass down to your children or grandchildren? In such a case it may be preferable to have shares that are easier to distribute than pass over ownership of a number of houses. We will look later on at reliefs available to pass down businesses and avoid Inheritance Tax.

Exit Strategy

What's your long-term plan and what's your exit strategy? While your exit strategy may be through the front door in a box, consider, as above, why and who are you buying property for? If it is to see you through to the end of your life, and you are happy to die with a £1,000,000 worth of property and £750,000 worth of debt, it will be much easier to keep extracting the cash if the assets are held in your own names.

Tax Tip

If you are not relying on the income, are a higher rate taxpayer and are creating wealth for the future, shelter that within a limited company. Draw down dividends when your income is not exposed to higher rates of tax.

CHAPTER 7

Avoiding Capital Gains Tax

7.1 Introduction

Capital Gains Tax (CGT) is a tax on the gain you make when you sell or otherwise dispose of an asset. You usually dispose of an asset when you no longer own it – for example, if you:

- Sell it

- Give it away

- Transfer it to someone else

- Exchange it for something else.

Capital Gains Tax is one of two significant capital taxes for any property investor, the other being Inheritance Tax. In both cases, the tax payable is being driven by the capital value of the property.

Please don't forget the distinction and the debate we had earlier between *investing* in property and *trading* in property; this section applies where you are looking to buy to hold, or have bought to hold and are now disposing of that property.

If you bought to flip, and go down this route you will find yourself in very hot water.

A capital gain arises on the disposal or part-disposal of an asset or part of an asset. Whilst here we are concentrating on property, the disposal of shares or antiques or other assets would represent a capital gain. Put simply: Net sale proceeds less base cost equals capital gain.

When a property investor comes to sell an investment property the sale **may** lead to a CGT liability. (Of course, any tax liability will naturally reduce the overall proceeds and, thus, the gain.)

Why 'may'?

Well, there are numerous reliefs and exemptions available – and also fantastic tax-planning opportunities that exist and which we will need to explore in in this chapter. (Incidentally, how many of you ever thought that you would hear 'tax' and 'fantastic' in the same sentence?)

Used correctly, these reliefs and careful planning can lead to significant tax-free gains. And you'd all like some of that, wouldn't you?

7.2 Some Basics

Before we get into the specifics let's have a look at some of the basics that underpin everything. Capital Gains Tax is payable in the UK by:

- Individuals who are UK resident or UK ordinarily resident

- UK resident trusts

- Non-resident persons trading in the UK through a branch or agency.

Non-residents, unless caught by the third point above, are generally exempt from Capital Gains Tax. This is a chapter about Capital Gains Tax and the subject of *residence*, *ordinary residence* and *domicile* can be quite extensive; given that the majority of readers are likely to be UK residents and the complexity of the subject we'll just say that the only way to establish whether you are resident, ordinarily resident or domiciled is an examination of your own personal circumstances in great detail. Professional advice is needed.

For now, and as a general rule:

- You are *resident* in the country in which you live

- You are *ordinarily resident* in the country in which you are usually resident

- You are *domiciled* in the country where you were born or where your nationality lies.

So if you have British parents, have lived in the UK all of your life then – most probably – you are resident, ordinarily resident and domiciled here. Phew!

Rates and Allowances

Each tax year nearly everyone who is potentially liable to Capital Gains Tax gets an annual tax-free allowance – spookily known as the 'Annual Exempt Amount'. You only pay CGT if your overall gains for the tax year (after deducting any losses and applying any reliefs) are above this amount. The annual tax-free allowance therefore allows you to make a certain amount of gains each year *before* you have to pay tax.

In 2013-14, the annual exempt amount is £10,900; thereafter, the following CGT rates apply:

- 18% for basic rate tax payers

- 28% for higher rate payers.

Essentially any capital gains are added last to your total income and taxed appropriately.

Inflation and common sense would suggest that, each year, the Annual Exempt Amount should increase. That has not, sadly, always been the case and a 'stealth tax' is to simply keep the allowance the same and watch inflation erode its real value, as happened between 2011/12 and 2012/13 where it remained at £10,600. Current (and past) rates can be found here:

http://www.hmrc.gov.uk/rates/cgt.htm

Separated couples will still be considered as 'connected persons' and divorced couples only become unconnected for tax purposes once the decree absolute has been granted. Tax is always paid on the 31 January following the year of assessment. So if a gain is made during the tax year 2013-14 then the tax will be due 31/01/2015.

So What is a Capital Gain?

A capital *gain* arises on the disposal or part-disposal of an asset or part of an asset, in this case property. At its simplest, it is the positive difference (i.e. the 'profit') between what you sold it for and what you bought it for (with a few twists and turns along the way).

Equally a capital *loss* will be where the net sale proceeds are less than the base cost. A capital loss in one year may be offset against capital gains in that year, and then (if not fully used) carried forward to future years.

A 'disposal' is deemed to take place as soon as there is an unconditional contract for the sale of an asset. This is **not** the same as the completion date – so beware if you are disposing of an asset around the end of the tax year, 5 April!

Ripley exchanges on the sale of his property on April 4 2014 with completion 10 days later. This would put the sale into 2013/14 with the tax due 31 January 2015 and so bring forward the tax liability by 12 months than necessary. A simple delay to put exchange on 7 April, just three days later, would push the tax bill back to 31 January 2016.

Tax Tip

In certain circumstances on disposal there is deemed to be neither gain nor loss on disposal. For example, transfers between husband and wife, or registered civil partners, will be totally exempt from Capital Gains Tax.

This exemption takes effect from the date of marriage and continues for the whole of any tax year when they are living together.

Net Sale Proceeds

This will usually be the actual sum paid by the vendor, from which may be deducted the costs of disposal. These costs need to spent wholly and exclusively for the purpose of the sale, and typically would include agent's fees, advertising and legal fees.

Neary sells his house for £400,000 after incurring agent's fees of £9,600, Sunday newspaper adverts costing £2,400 and legal fees of £2,000. His net sale proceeds are therefore £386,000 (£400,000-£9,600-£2,400-£2,000).

Caution

There are a few cases where it is not appropriate to simply use the cash proceeds; the three most likely for readers of this book are:

- Transfers between connected persons

- Transactions not at "arm's length"

- Non-cash proceeds.

It will useful to look at each of these to avoid stumbling into a tax minefield.

Connected persons

Where an asset is disposed of to a 'connected person' then the *open market value* of the asset should be used and not the actual consideration.

Thomas gifts to his son his holiday home in Wales. His generous gift would mean that he had made a disposal for Capital Gains Tax purposes and, as the house was worth £250,000, (even though he bought it many years ago for £50,000) then that figure is the deemed sale proceeds. There are also Inheritance Tax and Stamp Duty Land Tax issues but not for this chapter.

Connected persons can basically be found in a pack of "Happy Family" playing cards and will include:

- Husband, wife or civil partner

- Mother, father or grand parent

- Son, daughter

- Brother or sister

- Mother-in-law, father-in-law, son-in-law, daughter-in-law, brother-in-law, etc.

- Business partners

- Companies under the control of the other party selling to any of the above

- A trust where there are beneficiaries listed above.

Transactions not at "arm's-length"

Whose arm, you might well ask? From the list above it is clear that any transaction would not be at arms-length because of the close relationship. Thus market value must always be used and not any consideration given or the value of the gift. Whilst it will be fairly clear when people are connected, with *unconnected* persons HMRC assume that a transaction is at arms- length and the onus is on them (HMRC) to prove that it was not at arms -length.

Situations where this may be relevant are:

- The transfer of an asset between people living together but not married

- The sale of an asset to an employee

- A transaction which is part of a series of transactions

- A transaction which is part of a larger transaction.

O'Driscoll and O'Donnell have been living together for years. O'Driscoll sells O'Donnell a house that he no longer needs. Its market value is £100,000 but he agrees to sell it for £75,000 in the hope that she can get it revalued to £100,000 and extract some cash, or maybe even sell it for £100,000. All things being equal it's an arms-length transaction though if

HMRC can prove that its real value was £100,000 from suitable comparables then they may be some tough questions to answer.

Tax Tip

Document why it was sold at a particular price and why you consider that to be market value or even get a professional valuation.

Non-cash proceeds

In certain cases cash may not be exchanged for the asset – in which case the market value of the asset in exchange for the asset sold will be used.

Williams sells his house to an investor who pays part in cash £200,000 and transfers a plot of land in the mining village with a market value of £75,000. Williams' deemed sale proceeds adjusted for any legal requirements will be £275,000.

Cost

In calculating any gain we need to deduct the cost of the asset. The higher the cost then, yes, the lower the gain and the resultant tax bill – but please don't incur cost just to save tax! The cost will be made up of:

- The actual amount paid for the property

- Incidental acquisition costs (legal fees and stamp duty if appropriate)

- Enhancement expenditure (the cost of any substantial additions to the property) *Note that repair costs which have already been claimed against your income tax cannot be claimed here!*

- Expenditure in preserving or, indeed, establishing title

- Interest and other costs associated to raising the original finance

- Survey fees incurred as part of the decision to buy.

Tax would not be so much fun if there were not so many things to be wary of – and just with sorting out net sale proceeds there are things to be aware of: establishing base cost, connected persons issues. We also need to wary of assets acquired before 1 April 1982, so look out for:

- Inherited assets

- Assets acquired from a spouse

- Assets acquired, but not at "arm's-length"

- Assets acquired with no cash consideration

- Assets acquired before 1 April 1982.

Inherited assets

On death, all assets are included in the value of an estate at market value at around the date of death. Please note that Capital Gains Tax does not apply on death though be wary of Inheritance Tax. It's often said that the best way to avoid Capital Gains Tax is to die but it's a rather drastic step and as indicated will trigger an Inheritance Tax issue.

Whilst valuing a quoted share is simply a quick look in the Financial Times on the date of death, for other items you may need to include an appropriate valuation from a surveyor.

Based on current experience you will have no problem in getting the property valuation as low as possible in today's climate.

Edwards inherited a house on the death of his brother which his brother had bought for £50,000. On Edward's death in 2001, this property had a market value of £100,000.

In May 2014 it is worth £200,000 and Edwards decides to sell. The base cost for his Capital Gains Tax computation will be £100,000, that being its value when he inherited it – not when it was initially bought.

Assets acquired from a spouse

Assets transferred between spouses are treated as taking place on a no gain/loss basis.

When or if the spouse comes to dispose of the asset they are treated as having taken over the original cost from the transferee.

Duckham bought an investment property in 2000 for £250,000. After spending £50,000 on capital improvements he gifted the property to his wife in 2005. Mrs Duckham extended the property further at a cost of £100,000 and sold the property in 2013 for £600,000.

Mrs Duckham's cost would therefore be £400,000 (original cost of £250,000 plus improvements of £50,000 and £100,000).

Note that the no gain/no loss rule does not apply on death, where

Inheritance Tax takes precedence – but look out later on for a nice CGT exemption.

Just to confuse matters slightly, Labour introduced taper relief in 1998 and, in 2009, abolished indexation relief. This was designed to take out inflationary gains in capital assets.

So if the asset was transferred before the abolition of indexation then the base cost would be adjusted upwards to take account of inflation. Thus, in the above example, if Duckham had bought the property before April 1992 and transferred it before 2008 any indexation would be added to the transferee's (Mrs Duckham) base cost.

Assets acquired, but not at arm's-length

Any transfer to a connected person is deemed to be at market value and thus this will be used when determining the base cost.

Assets acquired for non-cash consideration

Where an asset was acquired for a non-cash consideration then its base cost will be determined by the market value of the consideration given.

Wheeler sells his house to an investor who pays part in cash £200,000 and transfer a plot of land in the village with a market value of £75,000. His deemed cost adjusted for any legal purposes will be £275,000.

Assets acquired before 1 April 1982

If you owned the asset on 31 March 1982, the market value of the asset at 31 March 1982 should be used in your Capital Gains Tax calculations, instead of the actual costs up to that date.

Helpfully HMRC tell us that "You need to keep any records that will help you do this." If you were around in 1982 and held investment property you are to be congratulated if you thought "I must get a 1982 valuation for when I come to sell my property in 2013!"

In practice it will be worked back with the use of house price indices.

McGeeghan bought a house in 1975 for £12,000 and spent the princely sum of £1,200 on capital improvements thus making a total cost of £13,200. At 31 March 1982 the property was worth £45,000 and that will be the value used if or when the property is disposed of.

Any subsequent capital improvements can be added to the cost but regardless of what it was bought for the 1982 valuation is used.

7.3 Hold-over relief

If a person transfers an asset to another person for nothing, in other words a pure gift, and it is a disposal otherwise than by way of a bargain at arm's length, this is still a disposal for Capital Gains Tax. However, 'hold-over relief' will apply: essentially, the chargeable gain is postponed, usually until the transferee disposes of the asset.

Hold-over relief may be claimed for:

- Gifts of business assets

- Gifts of unlisted shares in trading companies, etc.

- Gifts of agricultural land

- Gifts which are chargeable transfers for Inheritance Tax purposes

- Certain types of gifts which are specifically exempted from Inheritance Tax.

How does hold-over relief work?

Gavin Hastings gives a house worth £50,000 to his brother Scott on 25 August 2012. It cost him £17,000. The chargeable gain is therefore £33,000.

If a claim is made by the Hastings brothers, Gavin does not have to pay tax on the chargeable gain, which is known as the 'held-over gain'. Instead, Scott's cost for the purposes of calculating his Capital Gains Tax liability on any future disposal of the asset, which would normally be its value of £50,000, is reduced by the amount of the held-over gain, £33,000, leaving a base cost of £17,000.

Just one note of caution, in that where hold-over relief has been given on the disposal of a house, there may be restrictions on the entitlement to private residence relief on a subsequent disposal.

What if Scott made some small payment for the asset? If you receive something for the asset, such as money or another asset in exchange, and its value is greater than your base cost for the asset, then, subject to allowable losses, you are immediately chargeable on the excess of the value of what you have received over the base cost. Only the balance is held-over.

Scott sells a house to his bother for £40,000 in June 2012. The property was then worth £81,000. It cost Scott £23,000. The chargeable gain before hold-over relief is £58,000 (£81,000-£23,000). If Scott and Gavin make a claim, then, subject to the availability of allowable losses, Scott is chargeable at once on £17,000, being the proceeds minus the original cost. The held-over gain is £41,000.

The relief must be claimed by both parties to work.

Note that if an individual transferee emigrates within six years of the end of the tax year in which the gift was made, and the asset has not been disposed of, they are chargeable on the held-over gain. If the transferee dies then normal exemption on death would apply: I told you that death was a good way to avoid tax!

7.4 Joint ownership

It's worth reminding you that in England and Wales two people (either husband and wife or two joint venture investors) can own property as 'joint tenants', where they both own an equal interest in the whole property; or as 'tenants in common' where each own separate and identifiable shares. So, which saves the most tax?

As *joint tenants* your capital gains will be divided equally between you as would rental profits. When one owner dies, the property automatically becomes the possession of the other owner as there is no defined share. Typically, a husband and wife may own property jointly – though owning *in common* presents more planning opportunities for passing wealth through the generations.

Rodber is thinking of disposing of an investment property that is sitting on a capital gain of £20,000 and a potential Capital Gains Tax bill (£20,000-£10,600) at 28% of £2,632.

He therefore transfers 50% to his wife and, thus, the whole gain is sheltered by using both parties' annual exemptions – and he has avoided a tax bill of £2,632.

To make such a simple exercise pass without any undue interest from HMRC, it would be prudent to make the transfer:

- Sooner rather than later

- Certainly before the property is in the estate agent's window!

- Well before the legal boys get involved.

This would also work where either partner in the marriage was paying Capital Gains Tax at 18% instead of 28% – plus, of course, it doesn't need to be a 50/50 split: use the rates and allowances to your benefit. As *tenants in common* each will have a defined share (say, 40% or 50%, not the lounge and the main bedroom!) belonging to them – which they can choose to dispose of as they wish on their demise; it will not automatically pass to the other joint owner.

Unless specified, there is a presumption that the shares are equal as will be the share of profit. However, there is nothing to stop ownership being split 50/50 and profit split being in disproportionate shares – even 90/10 – so long as the wishes are recorded in writing. Do bear in mind though that such an election is irrevocable, but there is nothing to stop this being done on a property-by-property basis.

Tax Tip

If you are a married couple and thinking of disposing of a property where there is a potential capital gain, transfer a share to the other spouse to make use of their annual exemption for CGT.

Tax Tip

If bought as a married couple and one of them is a high earner compared to the other, then put 90% in the lower income or even no-income partner.

7.5 Principal Private Residence Exemption (PPR)

I'm sure that all of you know, but it does no harm to remind you that you can avoid some CGT on a property if it has, at some stage, been classed as your only or main residence.

Indeed, if the property was your only or main residence throughout the period of ownership then the profit made on the sale of your main home – no matter how large the gain – is completely exempt from CGT and is covered by the PPR exemption. Nothing ground breaking there!

However, used correctly and combined with other reliefs – and the fact that, for some of this period, the property doesn't even have to be your main home – it is possible to generate significant gains; and, yes, they will be tax-free! Every unmarried individual and legally married couple is entitled to the principal private residence exemption for their only or main residence – and, even better, the PPR extends to cover the last three years of *ownership*.

Uttley bought a house in 2005. He lived in it and then moved out in March 2012. He did not sell it until March 2015 – the entire period of ownership and gain would be exempt and covered by the PPR.

There is no reason why this property could not be let out over those three years (and being a good responsible taxpayer Uttley would include the rental income, less all relevant costs on his self-assessment return) because the PPR always extends to the last three years of ownership. There is, of course, no need to sell the property after the three years; whilst you will no longer qualify for PPR there is, luckily, another relief coming that will assist with a tax free disposal.

Tax Tip

To be fully exempt from Capital Gains Tax and make use of the PPR it's important that: it became your only or main residence immediately on purchase, or it was your only or main residence at some point and you sold it no more than three years after purchase

If you can't tick either box then you will still get a proportion of the relief plus your last three years.

Marriage and the PPR

Besides the benefits described above for transferring assets free of Capital Gains Tax, marriage brings some great planning opportunities around PPR. The average age at which couples are getting married is steadily increasing, so the chances are that each party will bring a house to the relationship – and those getting back on the horse after a divorce could also have a house to add to the pot.

Leaving aside the debate over which house they live in, both will qualify for PPR so you will need to elect which property that will be. Remember that the last three years of ownership after you have moved out will also qualify, and, indeed, three simple steps should guarantee that you are able to take full advantage of all available reliefs:

- Put both houses in joint names

- Live in each property as a married couple

- Elect for the one with the greatest potential capital gain to be your main home.

Switching your PPR

As indicated above, an unmarried individual or married couple can only have one main residence that qualifies for PPR. So if you end up owning more than one property at the same time you may pay Capital Gains Tax *on at least one* when you sell.

You can nominate which one you would like treated as your PPR and thus minimise the tax charge on both properties by switching the PPR between them (think MPs, high London house prices and rural constituencies). You have two years from the date that you acquired the second property to tell HMRC which is the main residence – and, yes, you can change it if you want. It goes without saying that you choose the property most likely to make a bigger capital gain or the one most likely to be sold first.

Lord Wilkinson lives in a small house in Newcastle where he works. In December 2000 he buys a house in London for weekend breaks and the occasional visit to Twickenham. After a reflective five minutes in December 2002 he realises that his London house has shot up in value but the house in Newcastle has hardly moved. He therefore bangs off an election to HMRC before the expiry of the two-year period and elects for the London home to be his main residence.

In 2012 Lord Wilkinson sells his London house and moves to the South of France and sells his London home with any gain covered by the PPR exemption. If and when he comes to sell the house in Newcastle it will be covered by PPR exemption up until December 2002, plus the last three years of ownership.

Incidentally the house in France will still be available for PPR exemption as this relief applies to his main residence, leaving aside any issues with French tax for now.

If you invest in a buy-to-let property, let it and sell it, then it will never have been your main residence and thus you will miss out on claiming PPR and private letting relief (see below) on any capital gain that you made.

Tax Tip

Let the house out that was your main residence and move into a new property. As the let property was once your main residence, then the last three years are exempt from CGT. So, sell within that three-year period and there will be no liability. Even after three years private letting relief will potentially remove any gain.

Tax Tip

You already own an investment property that has been let out for a number of years. You've never lived there (after all, these are boxes to make us money, not palatial homes) so at present you will not be able to claim PPR or private letting relief. So live in the property before you sell and – simply by making the property your main residence, even for a limited time – you can claim PPR and private letting relief. See below for some top tips on demonstrating this to HMRC but, again, always be aware of the wider circumstances: if you live in a five-bedroomed house in a leafy suburb and relocate to a two-bed townhouse to try and claim PPR, you might struggle. But if your modus operandi is to let two or three-bedroom homes not dissimilar to the one you currently live in than that clearly would work.

Interaction with GAAR, the general anti-abuse rule

This is a complex example, with multiple moves and houses which – on the face of it – must be artificial solely to avoid tax. However, it comes straight from the HMRC Guidance notes – and for that reason R has not played rugby for the British & Irish Lions.

R is extremely wealthy and has several houses outside the UK in which she spends five months of the year with the rest of the time in the UK. She acquires a London flat and she makes a main residence election in respect of it.

Four months later, she acquires a country house in Surrey and makes a main residence election in respect of that instead. A year later, she acquires a country house and makes a main residence election in respect of that. Eight months' later she decides to acquire a Scottish estate as many of her friends enjoy countryside pursuits. She makes a main residence election in respect of that.

She divides the seven months she spends in the UK between her various residences, spending the week in London and the weekend in her country home and holidays in Scotland. Hence all of them are occupied as a residence. Dissatisfied with the London flat, a year later, she sells that and buys a larger house in Chelsea, again making a main residence election in respect of that.

Shortly afterwards, fed up with the British weather she sells the country home and purchases a property in the south of France instead. However, she does not make a main residence election in respect of the French property. Within the next two years she decides that she prefers France and sells all her properties in the UK.

With guidance from her accountant, R is likely to claim that once a property has been a main residence then the last three years of ownership will count — even though, with the changing the election, that property had ceased to be her main residence; and also claim that the properties can be disposed of free of CGT.

Do the means of achieving the substantive tax results involve one or more contrived or abnormal steps? Not really; R just couldn't decide where to live. The fact that the election is for a property which is not (viewed objectively) the centre of the person's life *might* be considered to be abnormal, but as this is the specific effect of the legislation, this would not be considered to be abnormal on its own. Nor is it considered that submitting an election or claiming a relief is itself an arrangement or a contrived step.

Buying properties that are occupied as residences and then using the main residence election is using a relief afforded by statute and is not an abusive arrangement. The legislation places no limit on the number of times the election may be swapped!

Do the tax arrangements accord with established practice – and has HMRC indicated its acceptance of that practice? Well, yes, I think they have. GAAR would not apply – albeit that the facts are quite extreme. R regularly changed her main residence election; properties are sold within 3 years and thus they are all free of Capital Gains Tax.

7.6 Portfolio building

Given that any gain from the principal private residence, and at least the last three years following occupancy, are exempt from Capital Gains Tax you may be able to see that it is possible to build up a portfolio of property and pay little or no CGT.

Let me share a simple example

Brown buys his first flat (Property1), assisted by the bank of Mum and Dad for the deposit in 2010. He moves in; it's a new build in Troon so needs no work doing and it's his main residence.

His job is going well, and he's some spare cash and, having invested in his property education, decides to buy another property. He buys another flat (property 2) in 2011 but this is a repossession and a right mess – so needs a decent refurbishment to make it habitable; within a year he has moved into Property 2.

Why within a year, you may ask? Well, HMRC recognising that some people buy a wreck with a view to moving in once refurbished (or, indeed, any move in to the new house may be delayed) allow PPR to be extended to cover any period of up to one year during which the taxpayer is unable to occupy a newly acquired house – either due to the need to finalise construction or unforeseen delay in selling the old property.

Back to the portfolio building.

In 2012, Brown buys property 3. He's getting better and wiser at finding a deal (must have done our training) and buys a house at auction. Again, it will need a good year to make habitable and suitable to his taste and again, just before the year is up, he moves into property 3.

So with a reflective five minutes in 2012 having just moved into his third house, he works out that:

a) *Property one will be covered by PPR until 2014*

b) *Property two will be covered by PPR until 2015*

c) *Property three is currently covered until he moves again.*

Also bear in mind that Private Letting Relief (see below) will extend available reliefs.

Though Brown may choose to hold onto any property a combination of PPR, private letting relief and annual exemption could result in disposing of a property tax free.

Beware HMRC

This example is a perfectly safe and sensible way to build your portfolio – but beware of the attention of HMRC, who may argue:

a) That you are carrying on a trade of property development and would overturn the PPR

b) That you are acquiring property with the sole aim of realising a profit.

HMRC may have a point – but, if you are each time moving up the property ladder into a better house in a better area, it would be hard to attack. The passing of time will also help the risk of a potential attack and – above all – be sensible: given that moving house is one of the most stressful things that you can do, don't move from no 6 in the street to number 8 and then on to number 10!

While it costs HMRC significant sums to launch an investigation (and thankfully the days of idle 'fishing trips' are now behind us), a successful investigation may generate them significant returns through lost tax, interest and penalties – so HMRC, like any business, concentrates its efforts where it is most likely to see maximum returns.

To assist in its task, HMRC uses technology to bring together information formerly based in district councils and which enables the comparison of data collected such that, for example, an HMRC inspector can request a search to provide an historical list of all properties purchased by a landlord or, in some cases, members of the landlord's family!

This list can then be compared against declarations made on the Capital Gains Tax pages of personal tax returns. Properties sold within short timescales are thus easily identifiable and tax return declarations easily checked. Indeed, HMRC has had such success with its new system that it has formed a designated compliance unit tasked with targeting 'tax-evading' property developers and 'buy-to-let' landlords.

HMRC also compiles lists using information gleaned from other sources. Banks and building societies are required to provide details of accounts on which interest is paid over a certain amount. Such details may confirm the opening of a new bank account in which a large amount has been deposited. If this ties up with an entry on the Land Registry following the sale of a property, this could possibly mean that a chargeable gain should have been declared on a tax return. With that in mind, now might be a good time to flag up potential issues when making use of the PPR and what to do to keep HMRC at bay

a) It sounds daft, but it is essential that the property concerned is genuinely your private residence

b) There is no rule as to how long you should occupy the property – but you need to *live* there, so:

- Get all utilities in your name

- Be on the electoral roll

- Tell HMRC!

- Tell banks and credit card companies

- Inform family and friends

- Furnish it

- Don't move in and then try and sell or rent until a reasonable passage of time has passed. Always consider how you would respond to an investigation; given that HMRC might assume profit was the sole motive for your decision to move or sell, how would you allay their concerns?

Yes, I know the MPs have done it but let's be more thoughtful and less profligate with the nation's finances.

7.7 PPR and Developing Your Own Home

The PPR is a very handy way to ensure massive tax-free gains – and very useful given the rapid increase in house prices over the years; so how about extending and expanding the family home, adding value to maximise that tax-free gain.

All well and good, but just be careful. We can all agree that extending our own home either upwards or outwards for our continued enjoyment will cause no problems if we come to sell and we can enjoy the PPR exemption.

Remember, though your intention is everything. If you alter your house with the express intention of adding value before you sell then you may find that HMRC take a very dim view. The question, as always, is how do HMRC prove there was a profit motive and disallow a part of the gain? In practice it's very hard but not impossible – and will usually be spotted by actions of the taxpayer or even their neighbours.

Leonard moved out of his home when it was valued at £600,000 and moves into his new home. He knows it was around £600,000 as he had been marketing it for £625,000. As the property had not sold he was advised that, for the area, a fifth bedroom would add value and ensure a sale. £50,000 later, the east wing has been extended and the house sells for £700,000; Leonard relies on the PPR exemption as it's still within three years of moving out.

HMRC would deem that the extra profit of £50,000 is a capital gain and seeks to recover tax on that at 18 or 28%, maybe adjusted for his annual exemption. If Leonard had done the work before he moved out then the whole gain would have been tax free.

Similarly where there is one house split into two, any PPR will be restricted

As indicated above some people like to buy a wreck and renovate. Any added value, and thus profit, would be covered by the PPR but again be sensible and reasonable. At the risk of repeating it don't buy, renovate and move on every six to twelve months. It's obvious and could have massive tax implications

Mr & Mrs Quinnell bought their house for £100,000 and spent £25,000 renovating the property. No sooner has the project finished than it is on the market and sells for £175,000; they move to another wreck, having pocketed £50,000 less legals and admin expenses.

All seems sweetness and light and they complete their self-assessment return. An enquiry from HMRC (possibly triggered by the fact that the return shows yet another new address) reveals that they have bought and moved house within the same area six times in the last six years. They now have a tough job on their hands convincing HMRC that they moved for personal reasons; sadly, they fail to convince HMRC that they moved for legitimate reasons.

Not only do they kiss goodbye to the PPR, HMRC deems them to be trading in property and will look to collect tax on the profits made along with National Insurance.

Any calculated profits are income and would be added to their income for each tax year at their highest rate of tax, potentially 50%. For good measure, HMRC will want interest and penalties.

So please be prudent and thoughtful; as always, seek advice from a professional as to the possible tax implications. There may be good reasons to argue why the PPR exemption should apply – but if HMRC chooses to argue that it was done with a motive of profit, you or your accountant need to be prepared to argue this.

7.8 Making use of the Garden

The general rule is that where a house has a reasonably normal-sized garden, maybe a garage and a shed, then there will be no argument that any sale would be covered by the principal private residence exemption. But what about where the garden has substantial grounds and you fancy disposing of some of the land.

The general rule is that grounds are deemed to form part of the property where they do not exceed half a hectare (or 1.235 acres) (including the parcel of land on which the actual house is built). After this it becomes complicated and you need to argue that the additional area that is classed as garden is required, in the words of HMRC as "for the reasonable enjoyment of the dwelling house as a residence".

Well, that's crystal clear then! Just to add to the confusion, there is no clear definition and so case law and the learned opinion of judges comes in to play; typically, issues will be decided on a case by case basis.

That said, there are still some sizeable tax-free gains to be made if you get all your ducks in order so, in quick succession, here are some top tips:

- Do not sell your house and then the development plot

- Do not fence off the development plot from your garden

- Please use the development plot for your own use, be it tennis court, croquet lawn or simply a perfect lawn

- Please do not let the land lie abandoned and unloved.

Any of the above will simply wipe out your PPR for the piece of land earmarked for development – and also remember the 1.235 acres.

So simply sell off the piece of land. With massive forethought you may have obtained planning permission many years ago which is great as that clearly will add value to the land. However, please don't simply obtain planning permission and then sell the land. Remember that your intention is everything – so if you acquired permission with a view to selling, then you are going down the trader route; any capital reliefs that would otherwise be available will simply disappear.

Maybe even better, follow this strategy and top tax tip:

- Hold onto the plot and develop yourself

- Sell your old house (remember that you have three years to sell with the PPR)

- Genuinely use the new house as your principal residence

- DO NOT simply sell the newly developed house or you will fall into the trading trap: intention really is everything.

7.9 Private Letting Relief

As indicated above, if at some stage you have let your main residence (or indeed part of your home) then you can claim private letting relief. Helpfully, it makes no difference if you let the property out before or after it became your main residence.

The calculation is the lower of:

- The actual amount of PPR

- £40,000

- The actual gain before letting relief is set off.

Such a simple calculation is worthy of a demonstration.

Calder bought a house in September 2001 for £126,000. He lived in the property for two years and then moved away for work and chose to let out the property for a further nine years, when he sold the property for £225,000 in September 2012. In all, he owned the property for eleven years. Ignoring legal and selling costs, for the purpose of this example he is sitting on a gain of £99,000.

Firstly we calculate his PPR. He has owned it and lived in it for two years and can claim the last three years so his PPR will be 5/11 of £99,000 or £55,000.

As £40,000 is below £55,000 (the actual amount of PPR) and also £44,000 (the actual gain before letting relief, £99,000 - £55,000) Calder can deduct a further £40,000 from his calculations.

So now the taxable gain is £4,000 (£99,000-£55,000-£40,000). As that amount is below the Annual Exemption there will be no tax Capital Gains Tax to pay. If he'd bought the property as an investment – his tax bill would have been £27,720 (28% of £99,000).

Tax Tip

If the property is bought in joint names, then the husband and wife or registered civil partner can each claim the private letting relief. So the smarter ones amongst you will appreciate that that represents £80,000 worth of gain on which you can avoid CGT!

Tax Tip

The private letting relief calculation needs to be made for every property which has been your only or main residence at any time during its ownership. So, if desired or needed, you could sell two (or even more) homes that you have at some stage lived in, and collect the letting relief of £40,000.

Even better if you have followed the tax tip above then that's £80,000 per property on which you can avoid CGT. Happy days!

7.10   The Kids are Alright!

As explained above, every individual can have a main residence and therefore can claim PPR and, yes, that includes the children! Leaving aside the emotions invested, and the financial burden of them being a money pit for the first eighteen years (and probably a few more to come) once they get to the age of eighteen why not make use of *their* PPR – either by enabling them to buy a house in their desired town of further education, or simply to get them on the property ladder (and out the house).

This comes with a wealth warning! To do it properly will require you to (a) give away the deposit, (b) act as a guarantor and (c) forfeit any capital growth which will go to your children – but that at least will be covered by their PPR.

The kids must be on the deeds i.e. have legal title to the property, which is why this comes with a wealth warning; the property cannot be for your use and control. There may also be a potential Inheritance Tax issue, with passing wealth down to the children – though these will be avoided if you survive for seven years, at which point it will become an exempt transfer. In fact, the kids moving out may increase, not shorten your life expectancy!

> **Tax Tip**
>
> **The cash deposit given must be done so with no strings attached and with no contractual obligation to repay the money or indeed a share of any proceeds.**

That said, when Jeremy or Jemima ultimately sell the house and move up the property ladder, there is no reason of course why they can't make a generous cash gift back or maybe treat Mum and Dad to a very special holiday...

This is a book about property – but if you are in business and trade through a limited company and want to know ways to have private school fees and/or university fees paid out of pre-taxed income then please do email Iain@iainwallis.com.

CHAPTER 8

Other Taxes and Tax Points to Consider

8.1 Stamp Duty Land Tax (SDLT)

This tax is payable when there is a transfer of property. Whichever vehicle you choose to trade through, and whether you are a property developer or a property investor, then the same rates will apply – in virtually all circumstances.

SDLT rates for residential property

The rate that applies for all freehold residential purchases and transfers and the premium paid for a new lease or the assignment of an existing lease is (2012/13) as follows:

Purchase price/lease premium or transfer value	SDLT rate
Up to £125,000	Zero
Over £125,000 to £250,000	1%
Over £250,000 to £500,000	3%
Over £500,000 to £1 million	4%
Over £1 million to £2 million	5%
Over £2 million from 22 March 2012	7%
Over £2 million (purchased by certain persons including corporate bodies), from 21 March 2012	15%

It's not a particularly pleasant tax and HMRC simply help themselves to your wealth simply because you choose to purchase a house. As can be seen above, the rates become quite penal and the amounts payable can be considerable.

It's important to bear in mind that if the value is above the payment threshold, then SDLT is charged at the appropriate rate on the whole of the amount paid. Seems obvious but an example for clarity: A house bought for £130,000 is charged at 1 per cent, so £1,300 must be paid in SDLT. A house bought for £350,000 is charged at 3 per cent, so SDLT of £10,500 is payable.

An even more extreme example would be a house sold for £250,000 which would attract a duty of £2,500 (1%); but a house sold for just £1 more, at £250,001, would attract (if that's the word!) duty of £7,500, at 3%. So it would actually cost you £5,000 to pay one pound more for a property.

These thresholds are important and the smarter amongst you will have spotted that negotiating around stamp duty thresholds is very important. Suppose that you have viewed a house on the market for £140,000. You know now that you will have to add an additional 1% to the purchase price, so if you could negotiate and get that below £125,000, you would grab a bargain and also save SDLT. So a clever investor should be able to negotiate prices around the stamp duty thresholds.

Very often little 'vacuums' in the market are caused around this. OK, so saving £1,400 in SDLT is not huge but what if you were negotiating around the £250,000 mark? Do you want to pay 3% of £260,000 or 1% £249,950? That's a potential saving of £5,300 to be used for other and better things.

Sometimes the vendor just won't budge on total price, but they might agree a separate purchase for the moveable fixtures and fittings. That *may* work and this will be covered later – but for now, be aware that because of the potential savings to you and loss of tax revenue, HMRC tends to look very closely at transactions around the thresholds.

Tax Tip

Typically property investors are buying to hold – but there may be the odd occasion when you chose to sell a property.

Now with the boot on the other foot, you are aware of all the Jedi mind tricks that you used to secure yourself a bargain so what can you use to maximise your sales price?

We all like a deal so, maybe you could offer to pay the stamp duty on any agreed price. Yes, the tax will still be payable – but the mind works in mysterious ways: people love to feel they are getting something for nothing. You have a house for sale in excess of £150K. Your prospective purchaser offers you £140K, so you reply "How about you offer £150K and I'll pay your stamp duty." Sale agreed! The stamp duty which you pay is £1,500 and you didn't drop your price by 6% (10,000/150,000).

Higher rate for corporate bodies

From 21 March 2012, SDLT has been charged at 15 per cent on interests in residential dwellings costing more than £2 million purchased by certain 'non-natural persons'.

What with good reason you may ask is a non-natural person? This is not your mother-in-law – but, typically, will include companies, collective investment schemes and all partnerships with one or more members who are either a body corporate or a collective investment scheme.

There are exclusions for companies acting in their capacity as trustees for a settlement and property developers who meet certain conditions. But this is a topic far too involved and complex for this tile, which is looking at simple strategies to avoid tax on your property income. As with everything in this book, seek professional advice before proceeding.

Linked transactions

This is a very useful relief where transactions include the acquisition of interests in more than one dwelling.

Where the relief is claimed, the rate of SDLT which applies to the consideration attributable to interests in dwellings is determined by reference to the amount of this consideration, divided by the number of dwellings (i.e. the mean consideration attributable to the dwellings). This is subject to a minimum rate of 1%. Be aware that this only applies to residential property.

The rate of SDLT which applies to the consideration attributable to interests in land other than dwellings (if any) is the rate which would apply in the absence of the relief.

Squire purchases the freehold of a new block of 20 flats for £2.5 million.

There is no head lease and none of the flats is subject to a long lease. On the face of it he is looking at a consideration of £2.5 million and thus SDLT at 7% – a cool £175,000.

This transaction is a relevant transaction for the purposes of the relief as it involves the acquisition of more than one dwelling – the 20 flats – so the freehold is treated as if it were interests in the individual dwellings. The chargeable consideration, divided by the number of dwellings, is £125,000. This is below the *normal* 0% SDLT threshold – but the minimum rate of tax under the relief is 1%. The tax due is therefore 1% of £2.5 million , which is £25,000 – representing a saving of £150,000!

Ok, so we may not all aspire to buying large blocks of flats, so here's another example.

For whatever reason Telfer decides to buy a new build. Now we all know that you don't buy new build because you are paying the builder his profit but stick with the example.

Telfer agreed a price of £575,000 with the builder, so he's looking at 4% stamp duty which works out at £23,000. However, within this development are some two-bed houses at a price of £100,000 that he knows will let out easily – so he makes a cheeky offer and says "If you can agree £75,000 each, then I will take two."

So now Telfer's buying three houses for £725,000 – or an average purchase price of £241,666. This is subject to 1% stamp duty and he pays £2,417 and saves himself a cool £20,583.

The same trick could also apply where the property is not new build. Say that you've met an investor who's fed up with the buy-to-let market and wants to get rid of his portfolio. Leaving aside the potential capital gains issues, you could take any number of properties off him and they would be averaged for SDLT.

Fixtures and fittings

At the start of this section we touched on the way stamp duty changes at various thresholds – and the importance of keeping below a threshold if at all legally possible.

It's important to understand that *fixtures* are part and parcel of the house that you are purchasing and will attract SDLT – so you can't avoid SDLT by agreeing with the vendor to pay via a separate contract for the kitchen, bathroom etc.

On the other hand, *moveable fittings* are not part of the fabric; as the name suggests, they are 'moveable'. No SDLT will be payable for any items such as carpets, furniture, curtains and white goods, so if you like the current carpets, curtains and the huge American fridge that is too big for the removal company to shift, along with the 50" flatscreen TV, then it is possible and acceptable to agree that part of the agreed purchase price be for these items and thus reduce SDLT – or, in certain cases, shift it to a lower level or remove it completely.

To move from 3% to 1% around the £250,000 mark would wipe out £5,000.

Now, I appreciate that with some of the stock that you will be buying the last thing you want to do is hang on to the carpets – but if you can agree a price and that saves you SDLT it's worth a negotiation or two. After all, it makes no difference to the vendor, who still receives the same price - simply as two tranches.

However you must be reasonable. As I alluded to earlier, HMRC naturally takes an interest in all transactions which are just below SDLT thresholds. Remember that it is only moveable fittings that you are purchasing this way and, while there is no actual limit to what the vendor and buyer agree, it needs to be proportionate to the house – and capable of substantiation if HMRC requires it. HMRC's default position will be that you are trying to abuse the system - it will be up to you to persuade them otherwise!

8.2 National Insurance

If you are employed you will, assuming that you earn enough, pay Class 1 National Insurance and this will be deducted from your salary each month.

If you are self-employed you will pay Class2 which, in theory, goes to provide you with a derisory state pension – which is why you are investing in property. This is paid weekly though is normally collected by monthly direct debit. You will also pay Class 4 National Insurance, which provides you with nothing – so is basically a tax with a different name. This will be paid through your self-assessment return in equal chunks in January and July. The current tax rates are set out here:

http://www.hmrc.gov.uk/rates/nic.htm

So, what impact does that have on your property income?

Rental income is not classed as 'earnings' and therefore the rental income of a property *investor* is not subject to National Insurance of any class. Where you have property *trading* income your income will be subject to Class 2 and also Class 4 National Insurance.

8.3 VAT

Gordon Strachan, after another defeat, was asked for a quick word: "velocity," he replied and walked off! So here are a few quick words about VAT – not so much about *avoiding* it, as it is frankly impossible to avoid; more about some things to be aware of.

Domestic property

A property investment business does not need to register for VAT as the letting of property is an exempt supply, so the good news is that you don't have to become an unpaid collector of VAT every quarter. However, the downside is that any VAT incurred on your expenses can never be recovered.

If you run a deal packaging company, then it may be possible to register for VAT, even though your turnover is below the registration level; you can then reclaim the VAT on your associated costs – though you will now have to charge VAT to your clients, which may in turn make you more expensive.

If you run a property management company, then those services will be standard rated. You have the choice to register if below the threshold, to enable you to reclaim VAT – though again this is likely to make yourself more expensive to the end user, the landlord. (Incidentally, when my agent hit the registration threshold I simply asked for a reduced agency fee so I was no worse off!)

The letting of holiday accommodation will be standard rated.

The sale of residential property is an exempt supply so, again, the VAT incurred on any contractors' costs for work undertaken cannot be recovered. Where, however, the work is deemed to be a conversion then I have some good news.

Conversions

A reduced VAT rate of 5% applies where building work is carried out on a residential property *and the work results in a change to the number of dwellings in the property*, so you can:

- Turn one house into several self-contained flats

- Reverse that and turn self-contained flats back to a large house

- Knock two semis together to form one large house.

In all of these circumstances you will pay VAT at 5%. Even better, for those of you eyeing commercial premises, conversions into residential property will qualify for this reduced rate.

Commercial property

With commercial property there is what's called an 'option to tax', on a property by property basis. What that means is that the landlord can decide whether the rent is standard rated or zero rated. So if you opt to tax, then you can recover VAT on any expenses incurred; if your tenant is VAT registered then they can recover the tax paid and no one is any the worse.

Where it may go wrong is where you have a tenant who is *not* VAT registered and thus unable to recover the VAT; in these circumstances you are likely to be more expensive than other properties.

And beware that, where you have exercised the option to tax to recover VAT on some expenditure, any eventual sale will be at standard rate. This is where it could get expensive, as SDLT is calculated on the purchase price plus the VAT! Once again, planning and thinking ahead is the key to good property investment

8.4 Child Benefit Tax Charge

You may be liable to the High Income Child Benefit charge if you, or your partner, have an individual income of more than £50,000 and one of you gets child benefit. It may also apply if someone else receives child benefit for a child who lives with you. The amount of the tax charge will depend on the amount of:

- Child benefit entitlement

- The level of your 'adjusted net income'.

The amount of the tax charge will differ according to whether your income is:

- Between £50,000 and £60,000 *or*

- £60,000 or more

'Adjusted net income' is total taxable income less certain tax reliefs; to work this out is a simple four-step formula!

Step one: work out your 'net income'

Add up your taxable income, and include:

- Income from employment (including any company benefits)

- Profits from self-employment

- Taxable social security benefits

- Pensions (including the state pension)

- Savings, dividend and rental income.

Then deduct any reliefs that may apply:

- Payments made gross to pension schemes - those have been made without tax relief

- Trading losses, for example trade loss relief or property loss relief.

Step two: deduct Gift Aid donations

If you made a Gift Aid donation, take off the 'grossed-up' amount - what you paid plus the basic rate of tax. So, for every £1 of Gift Aid donations you made, take £1.25 from your net income.

Step three: deduct pension contributions

If you made a contribution to a pension scheme where your pension provider has already given you tax relief at basic rate, take off the 'grossed-up' amount – what you paid, plus the basic rate of tax. So, for every £1 of pension contribution you made, take £1.25 from your net income.

Step four: add back tax relief for payments to trade unions or police organisations

Tax relief of up to £100 is available if you make payments to a trade union or police organisation for superannuation, life assurance or funeral benefits.

Simples!

Laidlaw's total taxable income is £60,000, made up of:

- *Income from employment: £55,000*

- *Bank interest: £5,000.*

Laidlaw makes private pension contributions without tax relief of £4,750 so Laidlaw's net income is £55,250 (£60,000 less £4,750). He makes Gift Aid donations of £1,000 so he can take £1,250 off his net income - £1,000 plus £250, the value of the basic rate tax.

Laidlaw's adjusted net income is £54,000 (£55,250 less £1,250) and is used to work out the High Income Child Benefit charge.

Now we've established adjusted net income we can see what tax we will have to pay.

The tax charge will be 1 per cent of the Child Benefit paid, for every £100 of income between £50,000 and £60,000; and the tax charge will be less than the total amount of Child Benefit.

As above, Laidlaw's adjusted net income is £54,000. Laidlaw is entitled to Child Benefit, for two children, of £438 for the period from 7 January 2013 to 5 April 2013.

Laidlaw's tax charge will be worked out as follows:

- *Step one: income over £50,000 = £4,000*

- *Step two: determine the percentage rate to be applied to the result from step one. Here, £4,000 ÷ 100 = 40 (%)*

- *Step three: £438 x 40% = £175*

Laidlaw's tax charge will therefore be £175

If your individual income is £60,000 or more, the tax charge will be equal to the full amount of Child Benefit you, or your partner, are entitled to receive.

Dawson's individual adjusted net income is £62,000. He or his partner were entitled to receive Child Benefit of £438 for two children for the period from 7 January 2013 to 5 April 2013.

The tax charge will be £438.

There was much hot air and outrage and, frankly, obfuscation early in 2013 when this came in. Do I stop claiming child benefits? How do I repay? What if I over-claim?

Well, the simplest and easiest way will be to deal with this through your self-assessment return. To the extent that you owe HMRC then it will be collected on 31 January 2014; as explained earlier, it could even be collected through your tax code in 2014/15.

What can you do as property investor to avoid the charge?

Tax Tip

Arrange the property income in such a way as to keep both incomes below the £50,000 threshold and thus avoid the Child Benefit Charge.

8.5 Pensions

Maybe, like me, you first looked at property because your derisory pension statement predicted that, when you retire, you would be able to buy one – or even two – Mars bars. There are of course other ranges of confectionery.

Nevertheless that pension pot needs to be used to do something and if you have a SIPP (Self-Invested Pension Scheme) then this can be used to good effect. One initial problem is that SIPPs cannot invest in residential property – but there are plenty of areas where the funds *can* be invested and often to good effect, the main ones being:

- Commercial property

- Dedicated student halls of residence

- Hotels

- Residential care homes.

You will need to take specific advice from your pensions advisor before proceeding, but they are very tax efficient and also useful at releasing equity from your portfolio.

Greenwood owned a commercial property, the bottom floor of which was rented out to a café and upstairs to an Insurance broker.

Greenwood had bought this property a few years ago in his own name.

Greenwood transfers 50% to his wife to avoid the capital gain and then they sell the property to his SIPP which frees up money for him to go investing personally.

Tax Tip

Speak to your pensions advisor to make tax-efficient investments through your SIPP.

8.6 Overseas Property

I'm fortunate enough to be putting the finishing touches to this book from our ski in/ski out apartment in Switzerland. Even though it's the middle of summer, the views, if nothing else, are spectacular and inspire, plus it's nice to walk up stuff you skied down and think, "Wow, this is steep – how on earth did I ski down that?"

Like many of you who own overseas property it was definitely more heart than head – but it pays the bills and that's the most important thing. Yes I know it was off-plan and new build overseas in a non-English speaking country – but it worked, so cut me some slack!

So what about the tax? If you live and pay tax in the UK you *must* declare rental income from overseas property lettings on the foreign pages of your tax return. If you pay foreign tax on the income, you can usually get credit for this against the UK tax you have to pay on it. The amount of tax to be paid depends on whether you're 'resident' in the UK and 'ordinarily resident' or 'domiciled'. Oh no, not this again!

As explained earlier this will only affect a few people – so the easiest thing to do is nip along here and determine your status:

http://www.hmrc.gov.uk/international/residence.htm

I'm going to assume that you are resident, ordinarily resident and domiciled in the UK, in which case you will have to pay tax on the income from the letting *whether or not that income is brought into the UK*. This is known as the 'arising basis' of assessment.

Working out your taxable profit will be no different to calculating the profit for a property in the UK. Here, though, you can also deduct travel costs.

If you are fortunate to have more than one overseas property, losses from one overseas property are automatically offset against profits from the others – because all overseas property lettings are treated as a single business.

And if you make a loss overall, you can offset it against future years' overseas rental profits.

Note that *UK* and *overseas* letting businesses are taxed separately – losses from one can't be offset against the profits from the other.

If you are resident and/or ordinarily resident and domiciled in the UK, you will be liable to CGT *whether or not you bring the gains back into the UK*. You may also be liable to Capital Gains Tax depending on the laws of the country in which you hold the overseas property.

Where CGT is due you can usually get credit for foreign tax you've paid on the same gain under double taxation agreements – see here for more information:

http://www.hmrc.gov.uk/international/dta-intro.htm

Tax Tip

Just because your property is overseas, don't forget to tell HMRC.

Finally, if you like skiing down hills in the winter (with excellent links to Verbier and the Four Valleys) or walking up them in the summer months, or maybe you like cycling down hills or just enjoying the mountains you will be very welcome to visit Nendaz and enjoy the best of Switzerland here:

www.interhome.co.uk/switzerland/valais/nendaz/apartment-les-etagnes-ch1961.460.1/

8.7 Entrepreneurs' Relief

Entrepreneurs' Relief reduces the amount of the Capital Gains Tax on a disposal of qualifying business assets on or after 6 April 2008, as long as you have met the qualifying conditions throughout a one-year qualifying period – either up to the date of disposal, or the date the business ceased.

Qualifying capital gains for each individual are subject to a lifetime limit; for disposals on or after 6 April 2011 this currently amounts to £10 million. Entrepreneurs' Relief is available to individuals, and not to companies. And, as indicated elsewhere, it is not generally available to property investors – unless they have invested in qualifying furnished holiday accommodation.

However, it's not all bad news: you will recall we talked about how it *may* be available for property developers and traders. Equally, those investors who have managed to combine investment and trading, where the trading is the major part of the business.

Entrepreneurs' Relief must be claimed, in writing, and by the first anniversary of the 31 January following the end of the tax year in which the qualifying disposal takes place. The complicated statement simply means 'one year and 10 months from the end of the tax year in which the qualifying business disposal is made'.

Husbands, wives or civil partners are separate individuals and may each make a claim. They are each entitled to Entrepreneurs' Relief up to the maximum amount available for an individual provided that they each satisfy the relevant conditions.

To claim Entrepreneurs' Relief you have to meet the relevant qualifying conditions *throughout* a period of one year. This ends with the date when you disposed of the asset, or an interest in the asset for which you want relief, or the date when the business ceased, if that was earlier.

Tax Tip

The current allowance of £10,000,000 applies per person. So, if you are in the fortunate position of qualifying for Entrepreneurs Relief, it might be worth transferring to the spouse some of the qualifying assets at least a year before closing the deal.

A degree of crystal ball gazing is required, but we are all capable of managing our exit strategy.

CHAPTER 9

Avoiding Inheritance Tax

9.1 Introduction

It was Benjamin Franklyn who said that "There are only two certainties in life: Death and Taxes" and he was probably right. Whilst I can nothing about the former, I certainly can do a lot to sort out the latter. On the day that these two great 'certainties' collide then HMRC would naturally not want to let the opportunity pass to help themselves to a chunk of your hard earned wealth.

It's a fact that most people spend their entire life trying to accumulate a reasonable amount of wealth, to take care of themselves in their old age and then pass on any remaining surplus to their children or even grandchildren. It is somewhat unjust – or indeed downright wrong – that without careful planning and, yes, in certain cases a great deal of action throughout your life, then many families will ultimately face a huge and, frankly, unnecessary Inheritance Tax bill.

Now clearly if you are no more, you won't actually be writing the cheque payable to HMRC – but your estate will be paying Inheritance Tax on its overall value, be that your own home, your property portfolio, shares, cash at bank and valuables within the house.

Do you remember the opening lines of this book? If you do, then fantastic. The pain of paying unnecessary tax is still with you and, throughout this book, you've been noting where you've been leaving money with HMRC – and just what you will be doing in the future.

If you don't, then flick back now and remind yourself of what happened and how bad the pain was.

With the nil rate band currently £325,000, then most people can safely leave everything they have to their spouse or civil partner free from any Inheritance Tax plus, if you have no other dependants or potential beneficiaries to care about (and simply resent paying any unnecessary tax), you can simply leave it all to charity.

However, in the real world, most people do have someone they care about. Usually they have children or other family or friends whom they want to see benefit from the assets that they have built up in their lifetime; they don't want to see the government taking 40% of it away.

The mere fact that you are reading this book means that you are not like most people; indeed, you are extraordinary because, like me, you are investing in property. Maybe to increase your passive income, maybe to create wealth for your retirement – or indeed any number of reasons. Wherever you are on this property journey, and no matter what age you are, Inheritance Tax will be around the corner somewhere:

- If you are young and entrepreneurial, then it may impact on your parents or grandparents; you have a responsibility to flag up the problems that they may face

- If you are parents, then you need to be thinking about protecting your wealth and passing it to your children – and what about the impact on *your* parents

- If you are in your twilight years, well how do you protect your hard-earned wealth and pass it to your children and their children?

It really is never too early – or indeed too late – to start planning. Ever wondered why Inheritance Tax is called a voluntary tax?

The facts about the levels of Inheritance Tax paid are quite staggering. For the last year that figures are available, 2011/12, consider this:

- HMRC collected 2.91 billion pounds from Inheritance Tax

- That represented a 7% increase on the amount collected the previous year

- 20,000 individuals compared to 17,000 individuals paid Inheritance Tax.

Further, the fact that domestic house prices (particularly in the south east) are disproportionately high, allied to the fact that the chancellor has *frozen* the nil rate band at £325,000, will bring more and more people into the charge to Inheritance Tax.

Or will it?

Not for good reason is Inheritance Tax called a voluntary tax. That said, you need to take action to ensure that you do not pay tax unnecessarily throughout your entire life.

9.2 What is Inheritance Tax?

Inheritance Tax is not a tax that bites solely on death but on transfers of value. But what is a 'transfer of value', I hear you ask?

A transfer of value occurs whenever you dispose of something and, as a result, your total net wealth is reduced. Whether it be an asset or hard cash, if you give or transfer that to another person there has been a transfer of value.

Evans gives his collection of Porsche cars to his mate Edwards. The cars are valued at £100,000 so there has been a transfer of value and this is potentially liable to Inheritance Tax.

Why potentially liable?

Any lifetime transfers to an individual or trust are *potential exempt transfers* (PETs).

When a transfer of value is made, the PET clock starts ticking. What this means is that after seven years this transfer will fall off the schedule of transfers made and will be exempt from Inheritance Tax. *Only* if death occurs within seven years will Inheritance Tax apply – and even then there is tapering relief, the nearer that death happens to the seven-year anniversary the less relief is clawed back.

Rest assured that there are plenty of perfectly legal planning opportunities to avoid Inheritance Tax throughout your life. This will enable you to preserve the wealth that you, as a family unit, have generated (sometimes simply through house price inflation) and will enable you to pass that wealth down to generations to do what you or they wish – not want HMRC wants to do with 40% of it!

A university friend of mine has his widowed mum in a house which was bought for a modest sum in the 1960s; it is now worth a staggering £900,000. Does he want 40% of that to pass to the chancellor?

My uncle wrestled for hours over the decision to buy a new home in the early 70s for £15,000 as this would mean extending his mortgage. That detached house is now worth £1,000,000 – simply through house price inflation. Do you think he wants 40% to be given to HMRC?

It's a while since I mentioned this but, once again, let's nail this thing about tax avoidance. HMRC or indeed the Chancellor of the Exchequer may not like it, but it is perfectly legal.

Let me repeat that, because it is so important. Tax avoidance is perfectly legal. It is well-established that you can manage your affairs to legitimately avoid tax.

So what if the actions you take mean that you gain and the taxman misses out?

Ignorance is not bliss. Not knowing how you can legitimately avoid tax – or being scared of the taxman – is restricting your personal wealth. Everything throughout this book is 100% legal, safe to apply and should be being used by accountants up and down the land. If not, then you genuinely have the wrong accountant.

In this chapter on Inheritance Tax we are talking serious numbers. On your death, after the nil rate band has been used up, you are looking at 40% in tax. No ifs, or buts, or maybes.

Speaking as a tax accountant with more than thirty years' experience I can tell you that it is never too early to start Inheritance Tax planning and opportunities arise throughout as you progress through life. Though this book is essentially about property and tax, because I'm so passionate about you keeping your wealth I will add here some non-property tax planning to help preserve the family wealth. To start there are a number of simple exemptions that apply.

The **nil rate band** is probably the most important Inheritance Tax exemption for the vast majority of people. As the name suggests, an Inheritance Tax rate of nil is applied to the first part of your estate which falls within this band.

The current (2013/14) nil rate band, applying to deaths or chargeable lifetime transfers between 6th April 2009 and 5th April 2015 is £325,000. Yes, that's right! This has been fixed until 2015 and, naturally, this amount will be eroded by inflation. As most people's biggest asset is their home, and house prices do usually rise, so more and more people will be drawn into the Inheritance Tax net.

The nil rate band is available to each of us not just once a lifetime, but once every seven years! With careful planning, and starting as early as practically possible, significant sums can be sheltered from Inheritance Tax.

Inheritance Tax exemptions come in many different forms. Some exemptions are based on value; others on the relationship between the transferor and the transferee; still others on the nature of the transferee alone – and some even on the circumstances of the transferor's demise. Some exemptions have a general application; others apply only to lifetime transfers – and others only to transfers made on death. So you can see there is lots of potential complexity - and potential tax-saving scenarios. Ideally you need professional advice, but I'll do what I can to help you through the minefield!

9.3 The Circle of Life

Let's go through the circle of life and look at when and how we can make use of these exemptions to legally avoid this pernicious tax.

Let's get married

While most brides will be concerned about the wedding dress and plans for the big day, marriage is also a great opportunity to tell the family that, while getting married is an expensive business, it also provides a fantastic opportunity to do some Inheritance Tax planning.

We can get Mum & Dad to pay for the wedding – but gifts made 'in consideration of marriage' are exempt from Inheritance Tax, up to the following limits:

- Parents: £5,000

- Grandparents, great-grandparents, etc. : £2,500

- Bride to groom or groom to bride: £2,500

- Other donors: £1,000.

All of the above limits apply on an individual basis and the relationships referred to must be to one of the parties to the marriage. So the groom could receive £5,000 from *each* of his parents, plus £2,500 from *each* of his grandparents and £1,000 from all of his aunts and uncles – and the bride could receive the same from her family. Suddenly, an awful lot of cash has passed down a generation or two.

Now might be a good time to set up a trust for when the patter of baby feet comes along. It is certainly worth checking to ensure that you have a tax-efficient will.

Tax Tip

Use your wedding to remind relations to pass wealth down to you, tax-free.

Parenthood

Yes, once again it's time to review the will. In the unlikely event of your early demise, how will you provide for your children? What form of trust would you set up?

After that slightly morbid thought, and on a more positive note, parenthood might just concentrate the mind to, maybe, put some money into a trust for your child or children to pay for their education – or simply to move wealth from your estate to theirs. Your parents (your children's grandparents) can also pass wealth down.

Tax Tip

Consider setting up a trust to get wealth away from you and, maybe, your parents.

Adult Kids

No matter how old you are your mother can, and will tell you off, but once you reach the age of 18 then this opens up all sorts of possibilities. Passing wealth to someone under the age of 18 serves little purpose, unless it goes into a trust, as the capital is deemed to be that of the parents. Now might be a good time to talk about **the annual exemption**. The first £3,000 of *any* transfer of value in each tax year is exempt from Inheritance Tax; married couples each have an exemption. Further, this exemption may be carried forward for one year if not used in the previous year.

So parents can pass a total of £6,000 a year under the annual exemption – and, if not used the previous year, £12,000. It was, and remains, a particularly useful exemption, and one I was keen to tell my parents about when I was an impoverished trainee accountant. Sadly, this advice fell on deaf ears.

Tax Tip

Use your £3,000 annual exemption to pass wealth down to the family every year.

Let's look at how the nil rate band could be used on a seven-year cycle:

Assuming that no other transfers of value have been made, Andrew and Mrs Andrew each use their nil rate band and put £325,000 into a trust for their adult children on 5 April 2013.

Each subsequent year they put in £6,000 using the annual exemption (see above) so that by 5 April 2020 the value of the trust has increased to £692,000. (In actual fact it will be higher as the cap on the nil rate band should come off after 2015 but for ease I have ignored this.)

This £692,000 then drops off their Inheritance Tax clock, and thus this money has now passed tax free out of the estate.

On 6 April 2020 in the next tax year they rinse and repeat.

Were this cycle to be interrupted by a death then tapering relief on a sliding scale would apply, so the further you are down the seven year road, the less of the tax relief would be clawed back.

If you are wealthy enough, then lifetime transfers that are part of 'normal or habitual expenditure' will also be exempt. This is both very useful as, unlike the annual exemption, there is no upper limit and it enables significant sums to pass through the generations. So long as the payments are *regular, out of income* and leave the donor with enough to live on then they will qualify.

Carling, who works in the city, gives his two children, Jeremy and Jemima, £25,000 each at Christmas (and maybe Easter as well). As his annual salary plus bonus is just shy of £2,000,000, this transfer is really petty cash and the wealth passes tax free.

At a more modest level, and because she can, Granny gives her six grandchildren, who are all over 18, a cheque for £500 each month. During one year £36,000 will have passed out of her estate and potentially saved £14,400 Inheritance Tax.

Tax Tip

If you are fortunate to be in a position to make regular gifts from income, then make sure that you do.

Grandchildren

A theme might be developing here but, yes, you guessed it – it's time to review the will again. The key thing here is that you can now skip a generation to avoid two bites at your pot of wealth by HMRC. Say you pass £100,000 to your kids who on in turn pass to their children then we have two not one transfers of value. So pass direct to the grandchildren.

You may also want to consider setting up a trust so that the wealth passes to them when they reach the age of 18, or some later date.

Death

Let's assume that you have a valid will in place. If you don't and you die intestate then all sorts of complicated rules kick in and not necessarily to your benefit – so, if you do nothing else after reading this chapter, make a will!

As indicated above it may be useful to skip a generation, assuming that your children don't financially need to be a beneficiary.

Generally, all gifts to charity are exempt from Inheritance Tax. This covers both outright gifts and transfers into a charitable trust. A charity is defined as 'any body of persons established for charitable purposes only'.

Equally the following are exempt from Inheritance Tax:

- Gifts to housing associations

- Gifts to national bodies (e.g. British Museum)

- Political parties – though they must have at least two elected members at the last general election. So whilst leaving £1,000,000 to The Monster Raving Looney Party may seem no different to leaving it to one of the three main parties, sadly it will not attract tax relief.

There is also a complete exemption from any Inheritance Tax arising on the death of a person from wound, accident or disease contracted whilst on active military service.

So you can begin to see that there really is no need to just roll over and let HMRC help itself to 40% of your wealth. However, Inheritance Tax law is constantly changing. This means that no one can be sure of having avoided the tax until they have gone to meet their maker.

So (and I would say this, wouldn't I) in addition to taking professional advice when putting your plans into effect, you should also undertake a *regular* professional review to determine whether your planning remains effective.

As much of the exposure to Inheritance Tax comes from high property values, let's first look at the family home and then look at investment portfolios

9.4 The Family Home

Until the property portfolio has grown this is likely to be the most significant asset exposed to Inheritance Tax. While we can make use of the nil rate band of £325,000 (which can shelter £650,000 if you are married) that is not always sufficient with high house prices – particularly in the south east, though high house prices can be found all over the country.

Now some of you might be thinking well, I'll give it to the kids and live here until I die. All well and good – but you will fall at the first hurdle namely the 'gift with reservation' provisions. Put simply, you can't give the house to your children or whoever and continue to enjoy the benefit of that asset – or, for that matter, any asset.

Any gift where you retain a beneficial interest in the asset gifted are simply ineffective for Inheritance Tax purposes. In general terms, a gift is one with reservation if:

- The donee does not assume *bona fide* possession and enjoyment of the gifted property

- The gifted property is not enjoyed to the entire exclusion, or virtually to the entire exclusion, of the donor and of any benefit to the donor by contract or otherwise.

Windsor gifts his entire collection of Napoleonic swords to his son, but keeps them in the study so that he can still enjoy them at his home. Such a gift would fail because the son does not have bona fide enjoyment of the property.

Cotton gifts his row of holiday cottages to his daughter, but reserves the right to visit every summer. Again, this would fail under the second provision as it is not enjoyed in its entirety.

You could proceed and gift the family home and decide to pay the going rate for that particular size of property. That would get around the gifts of reservation but, in turn, throws up other issues:

- The kids will have to account for income tax on the rent received, with few expenses to offset it; that said, once the tenancy has started you could fully redecorate and re-carpet the house, assuming that you had sufficient funds

- You could be creating a Capital Gains Tax problem if the house rises significantly in value

- A benefit, however, would be that the rent paid would further reduce the value of your estate.

So it's probably back to the drawing board regarding the main home.

There are some measures with various pitfalls and degrees of complexity, which could include:

- Moving out the house and giving it away

- Selling up and giving away the proceeds

- Maximise the debt and give away the proceeds

- Sell at market value

- Selling up and investing in assets that escape Inheritance Tax

- Play happy families.

So let's look at each in turn, mindful of the fact that, in each case, you may need sufficient additional wealth – and not forgetting that, in certain cases, it will be a potentially exempt transfer and so the transferor will need to survive seven years.

Move out and give away

Provided you are of sufficient means and prepared to do so, you can simply move out and give the house away. Yes, we will need survival of seven years – but don't forget that with the PPR rules (see the Capital Gains Tax section) you have a further three years to give away the property. Depending on your circumstances you could buy a more modest house or simply rent a new property.

Move out and sell up

No one would deny that you need to be wealthy and cash rich to simply walk away, so a hybrid of the above would be to sell and then give away the cash to the beneficiaries. Again you would need to survive seven years and maybe buy a smaller, less expensive, home.

I wouldn't suggest offloading all the proceeds *unless you have guaranteed income from another source*, maybe a property portfolio. Plus, you never know how long you will survive for.

Maximise the debt

It may be that you actually quite like where you are living, but can't stomach the thought of losing 40% on your demise. Income and age levels permitting to get a mortgage, then why not max out the debt on your current house? Any debt will be deducted from your overall estate and, provided that the funds are not sitting in a bank account, will escape Inheritance Tax. Again we need seven years of survival and either give the cash away or spend it. However, don't forget that you need to finance the mortgage.

I hear that the young-at-heart now go on SKI holidays. Now before you picture Granny hurtling down a black run at Verbier that ski is 'Spend Kids Inheritance'! Some take the view that they had nothing passed down to them, so let's enjoy it while we can. Ever wonder why round-the-world cruises at premium prices are always sold out?

Maximise portfolio debt

Not only can you max out the debt on your main home, there is nothing to stop you stripping out as much equity as possible from your property portfolio. Sure, not all of the debt will attract tax relief and, yes, you need the ability to fund the interest – but there will be significant tax breaks. But with one very dangerous consequence. Let's explore this further.

Wood has one property in his portfolio with significant equity; for this example, say it is valued at £100,000 and was bought for £20,000. He knows that if he sells he will have a substantial capital gain – but he needs cash to add to his portfolio so, rather than sell, he gets tax free cash out of his one property. He therefore extracts 75% of the value by taking out a mortgage, and starts to go shopping, You will now know that, provided those proceeds are used in his property business, he will get 100% tax relief on the interest.

Over time the portfolio grows and grows, as does the capital value; the portfolio is now worth £3,000,000. He realises that he has created wealth – but he also has a potentially massive bill for Inheritance Tax and the thought of passing 40% to HMRC, whilst making him feel sick, also stirs him into action. Knowing that debt is deducted from the value of assets for Inheritance Tax he fires up his mortgage broker and gets a 75% loan against his entire portfolio so he now has property of £3,000,000, debt of £2,250,000 and equity of £750,000. Yes, some still exposed to Inheritance Tax but not as much as before.

All is going along swimmingly until there is a downturn in Wood's earnings; this coincides with a decrease in house prices. He needs to sell and knows that his best gain is on his first property, even though it's dropped from the £300,000 when it was last mortgaged. It sells for £275,000 and after clearing the debt (£300,000 × 0.75) and ignoring costs and agent's fees, he pockets just £50,000. (After costs it's probably less.) Even worse, he has created a Capital Gains Tax liability. This property was bought for £20,000 so represents a gain of £255,000 – which at 18% amounts to £45,900 or at 28% £71,400! At best he breaks even cash-wise; at worse he's out of pocket. Ouch!

A number of lessons:

- Speak to your accountant *before you do anything* as chances are they would have flagged up the potential problem

- Don't keep remortgaging if, at some stage in the future, you may have to sell a property or two

- Don't assume that house prices will always rise (or will be rising at the time you may need to sell)

- It may have been better to suffer the cashflow pain rather than sell the house and hang on till death (drastic but again a useful plan)

- He could have left the UK permanently and sold his properties free of Capital Gains Tax. That would require severing all ties with the UK. Plus he does not want to find himself in a country where the Capital Gains Tax regime is as bad or even worse than the UK. Note that before emigrating you must take professional advice to ensure that it is done properly.

Sell at market value

This is not dissimilar to simply gifting the entire property, though because a consideration has been paid by the children there is no transfer of value. There still remains the problem of passing the proceeds down through the generations. Also, bear in mind that a condition that you can occupy post-sale should *not* be part of the contract – so you could find yourself with a pot of cash, but no home!

Sell up or remortgage and invest in IHT-free assets

Shares traded on AIM (the Alternative Investment Market) attract 100% business property relief, so max out the debt or sell completely and invest the proceeds in AIM. Provided that these shares are held for two years they will be completely free from Inheritance Tax.

Happy families

You probably rejoiced the day that the kids finally move out of the family home, but things have now gone full circle and it's time to bring them all back together again and maybe save some tax as well. It would work best with a single child and one remaining parent but there's no reason why the whole family couldn't decamp under one roof. You just need enough wings to give everyone some space and, of course, all chip in for the running costs.

Put the property into joint ownership with one of the adult children and, so long as they live there, then it will be a potentially exempt transfer. It is, however, important that they actually live there; you will recall the steps needed to prove this to HMRC.

Be aware that this is almost 'till death us do part' – for if one or more of the children move out, the only way to avoid the gift with reservation would be for the parent to start paying a commercial rent, as in the example above.

Tax Mitigation Strategy

All of the above have various merits – but, possibly, the simplest would be a sale of your property, at full market value, to your children through a tax mitigation strategy. The benefits here are that:

- It can be used for the family home

- It transfers the value out of your estate to the next generation

- No need for a trust

- Consideration is an IOU

- Enables you to keep control of the asset

- You can still live in the property

- Low-risk tax avoidance scheme

All that is needed for this strategy to work is:

- Married/civil partnership

- Both parties to survive for at least seven years

- Need to be reasonably cash liquid.

So imagine, excluding all other reliefs, that your family home is worth £1,000,000. Do you want to pay 40% on death i.e. £400,000 – or do you want to pay fees to pursue a tax mitigation strategy. Yes, there may be some stamp duty considerations but, nonetheless, considerable savings. If you would like further information about this particular strategy please email Iain@Iainwallis.com .

9.5 Business Property Relief

I referred above to 100% business property relief and, provided that all the criteria are met, then it should be possible to obtain this and thus avoid Inheritance Tax.

Fantastic, I hear you say. What a great way to shelter my property portfolio!

Let's look first at business property relief – and then look at *why* we need to be a little more creative when it comes to property. You can claim business relief on:

- A business or an interest in a business

- Unlisted shares (shares that aren't listed on a recognised stock exchange), including shares that are traded on the Alternative Investment Market

- A holding of shares or securities that you own which give you control of a company, that are fully listed on a recognised stock exchange

- Any land, buildings, plant or machinery you own, used wholly or mainly in the business during the last two years before the business was passed on (or since your business acquired them if more recent)

- Any land, buildings, plant or machinery used in your business and held in a trust that you have the right to benefit from.

On the face of it that looks promising – until you discover that you can't claim business relief if:

- The business or company mainly deals with securities, stocks or shares, land or buildings, or in making or holding investments.

There are other situations but this is the most pertinent, as HMRC takes the view that simply holding property and collecting rent does not constitute a 'business' for business property relief – and they have case law on their side.

Well, you may think. They seem quite happy to collect tax from rental income that does not constitute a business. Yes, I have some sympathy for this view – but then whoever said that tax was supposed to be fair!

Business property relief may apply to furnished lettings but, in the main, simply holding investment property is unlikely to obtain any business property relief.

Well that's it, then. We might as well pack up! Don't be quite so hasty: a property *development* company that, by its very nature, will not be holding investment property will qualify – so that's a start. Maybe we could look at adding investment property to the company and working the two together. The legislation refers to 'wholly or mainly' but, as ever with tax legislation, fails to define 'wholly or mainly'. Is it based on turnover, asset values, gross or net profit? You decide.

If we have more than a simple 50/50 split (on any of these bases) then I would suggest it might be worth a scrap with HMRC, because if we have a business that develops and also holds property then we have game on!

Gravell & Guscott run a property development and property investment holding business. About 60% of the income derives from property development and, while HMRC would rightly argue that the holding of investments is a non-qualifying activity, it only represents a minority part and the main part (albeit 60%) is a qualifying activity. All of a sudden the whole of the business will qualify for Business Property Relief, including the investment properties.

Tax Tip

If you are a trader and an investor, make sure that the trading element i.e. the qualifying activity is more than 50%of the business turnover.

As indicated above you need to have held a property for a minimum of two years to qualify for business property relief and this, again, represents a fantastic opportunity to avoid Inheritance Tax.

Consider this: a business owner has built up a profitable and asset-rich business over many years but as it is essentially investing in property it is a non-qualifying business. If the owner can steer the business towards a qualifying activity then the opportunity to avoid Inheritance Tax presents itself.

Irvine, over many years, through his company has built up a sizeable property investment business. Recognising that there may be some tax issues he employs Irvine Junior. Irvine Junior believes that property development is more rewarding than holding assets and gradually steers the company towards this line of business. After two years and with more than 50% of the company's turnover coming from a qualifying activity, all the property in the company will qualify for business property relief.

Tax Tip

If you've built up your portfolio in a limited company then look at changing direction to secure business property relief.

9.6 Employee Ownership Trust

It may be that moving into development does not really float your boat. What else could be done to protect the value of your buy-to-let portfolio? At the outset we have a portfolio of property that won't qualify for business property relief or any other Inheritance Tax reliefs.

We may also have cash and other share investments.

Well, how about pursuing a simple tax mitigation strategy?

The purpose is to enable family wealth to be used to provide long-term benefits to children and grandchildren as a reward for working in the family investment business, rather than just 'handing over' the assets to them. It also allows accumulated family wealth to be retained by the family for the long term and, therefore, allows it to be used flexibly to benefit children and grandchildren in the future. It may be particularly suitable where there is a desire to prevent the next generation from dissipating family wealth, or to protect it from children's or grandchildren's spouses in the event of divorce or separation.

It enables control to be retained over the family wealth by the individual until succession, and thereafter to control how family wealth is applied to future generations. In addition, the family wealth is also largely protected from dissipation via future Inheritance Tax charges.

Essentially the process is as follows:

- Transfer value out of estate to a limited company

- Transfer a minimum of 50% of the shares in the company to an employee ownership trust

- Obtain immediate 100% relief from IHT

- No need for a seven-year survival

- Continue to control the assets and the income.

Yes there may be some stamp duty land tax and potential Capital Gains Tax considerations to consider, but these are significantly outweighed by the considerable savings. If you would like further information about this particular strategy please email Iain@Iainwallis.com.

9.7 Short Life Time Expectancy

Remember the lady at the start of this book? How an illness concentrated the mind with regard to the Inheritance Tax bombshell? Sometimes, life gets in the way and it's all too easy not to do things that we really know are important. After all, how many of you have not made a will!

Similar to the employee ownership trust, schemes are available where there is limited life expectancy; providing the donor has at least six months to live it is possible to avoid Inheritance Tax and pass the wealth down to the family. Again, there may be some stamp duty land tax and potential Capital Gains Tax considerations to consider but, again, considerable savings. If you would like further information about this particular strategy please email Iain@Iainwallis.com.

9.8 Capital Gains Tax and Inheritance Tax

To qualify as a Chartered Accountant you have to take professional exams; not surprisingly, these would include exams on taxation. When I qualified way back in 1984 you took PE1 and PE2. Whilst PE1 would tackle issues in the foothills of your tax knowledge, as sure as eggs are eggs at PE2 you would get a question involving both Inheritance Tax and Capital Gains Tax, as these two beasts collide.

You will recall within the CGT section that I said that death was particularly useful tax planning. That's not to be flippant, because it is. Why? Well, during your lifetime and the desire to transfer value out of your estate – and thus avoid Inheritance Tax – every lifetime transfer will give rise to a disposal for CGT, and the consideration will always be at market value. Only lifetime transfers of cash will escape CGT as cash acquired and cash disposed of will always be at market value.

So we have a conundrum:

- Avoid Inheritance Tax by making lifetime transfers *or*

- Avoid Capital Gains Tax by holding assets until death.

Lifetime transfers are made at market value, whereas on death the base cost will be uplifted to market value. In certain cases it may be better to suffer Capital Gains Tax at 18% or 28% given the potential saving of Inheritance Tax at 40%. Just to stir the pot of pain, stamp duty will rear its ugly head as well.

It really is 'a fine mess', demonstrated by looking at what is likely to be the biggest asset, the family home. You will recall the CGT section, where we looked at the family home and how, in the main, any disposal will be exempt from CGT – and earlier in this chapter we looked at what could be done to avoid Inheritance Tax by disposing of the family home.

Giving away the family home, which is a legitimate planning exercise will both remove any uplift on death and, if the transferees do not move in, then they will lose any main residence exemption.

So the mess will be:

- Avoid Inheritance Tax (which is hopefully *greater* than the potential CGT): seems reasonable

- Avoid Inheritance Tax (which is hopefully *no greater* than the potential CGT): score draw

- Avoid Inheritance Tax (which ends up being *less* than the potential CGT): whoops!

So, remembering the old adage about the tax, the tail and the dog – think your actions and the likely tax consequences through first!

9.9 Summary

You can begin to see that there really is no need to just roll over and let HMRC help themselves to 40% of your wealth. Yes, it requires careful planning and, yes, it requires action. Just to repeat "to know and not to do is not to know"! and you will be no better off than someone who has not yet bought this book.

Don't complain then if you end up paying 40% to HMRC by failing to take action.

Go here to see if you could save or avoid Inheritance Tax:

http://www.legallyavoidtax.co.uk/survey

Beware, though, as Inheritance Tax law is constantly changing. As mentioned before (and I would say this wouldn't I) in addition to taking professional advice when putting your plans into effect, you should also undertake a *regular* professional review to determine whether your planning remains effective.

Good luck in keeping your wealth from HMRC and please, please, don't write a cheque for £1.8 million to HMRC.

CHAPTER 10

Tax Investigations

Whilst this is a book about legal and legitimate tax avoidance, no harm is done in flagging up the pain and inconvenience – not to mention the huge amount of stress – caused if you try and beat the system.

HMRC raises several hundred tax investigations per year into the affairs of individuals, businesses and companies. The vast majority of these will have been risk-assessed by reference to documents previously submitted to HMRC, as well as information from third parties. (You would be amazed how useful a source of information a divorced party could be to HMRC so, yes, information is gathered from all sources.) In the main, however, it will be something that is out of the ordinary from the statistical analysis complied from all completed returns that will be the trigger. Some anomaly, something that 'doesn't fit'.

As part of HMRC's broader work to tackle tax evasion and avoidance, it has established taskforce teams to undertake highly focussed compliance activity into high-risk sectors across the UK. Current taskforces that may be of interest to those investing in property:

- Construction traders in the north west of England and Wales

- Landlords, owning or renting three or more properties, in the north west of England and North Wales

- Property transactions in London

- Property rentals in East Anglia

- Property rentals in London

- Property rentals in Yorkshire and north east of England

- The rental property sector in the south east.

It is highly likely that, where businesses fall within the individual taskforces mentioned above, HMRC will conduct unannounced visits to ensure that evidence of potential non-compliance is not destroyed. You have been warned.

This is a book about tax savings though it's worth knowing who may have you in their sights. As indicated earlier, if you have done nothing wrong then there is really nothing to fear but, unless you are very brave, do not tackle them alone. Seek professional help.

HMRC instigates tax investigations from three offices:

The local area tax office will deal with:

- Tax investigations into individuals

- VAT investigations

- PAYE investigations (also known as Employer Compliance Reviews)

- Code of Practice 9 – Contractual Disclosure Facility (CDF: a bit technical but all will be explained below) where the expected yield is less than £500,000.

Specialist investigations will deal with:

- Code of Practice 9 – Contractual Disclosure Facility (CDF) where the expected yield *exceeds* £500,000

- Large, complex or technical cases but where fraud is not suspected

- Insolvency tax investigations.

Just to repeat that it's not all doom and gloom, it is important to point out that the law does not require perfection. It requires that you take 'reasonable care' to get your tax right. We are now, and have been for a number of years, under self-assessment; it is for you to provide all the information and get your tax right.

If you make a genuine mistake and can demonstrate that you took 'reasonable care' no penalty will be due. Alas, there is no legal definition of 'reasonable care' so common sense will prevail and the facts of each case.

If you "forgot" that you sold a property and didn't declare a capital gain that's hardly reasonable care; but if, in the absence of a lost bill, you over-estimated some capital improvement costs when completing your tax return which was found to be excessive then you are unlikely to unleash the Harbingers of Hell at HMRC.

The things to consider are:

- Have you under-declared your tax liability?

- Have you over-claimed tax repayments?

- Have you failed to tell them that you are liable to pay tax?

Landlords, be Very Aware

I'm always amazed at how many people don't tell HMRC that they have a buy-to-let property because 'it didn't make a profit'. That may well be the case, but it is a new source of income and you need to tell HMRC because (to your advantage) you can agree any loss to carry forward and also if, through their trawl of the land registry, they find that you have not told them about a property they can investigate you and make your life hell.

Once an enquiry has been launched, considerable savings in the penalties handed out once any investigation is concluded can be achieved by prompt disclosure, prompt and full response to all correspondence and, yes, active co-operation in bringing matters up to date.

Needless to say HMRC rightly take a dim view if you try and play games or be evasive in your dealings with them. As indicated above, if you are involved in an investigation then seek professional help but, just so you are aware of how life can get tough if you evade – and hopefully to act as a deterrent to stay the right side of the law – here's what could happen.

For tax years up to and including 2007/08 HMRC will start with a penalty of 100% *of the unpaid tax*. So if they've found £10,000 worth of tax which was unpaid, you could be looking at a bill of £20,000 – plus of course they will charge you interest on the unpaid tax.

That penalty can be reduced; it starts at 100% of the unpaid tax, but is then reduced with reference to the following:

- **Disclosure:** The maximum reduction is 20%, but an additional 10% can be awarded in circumstances where an entirely voluntary disclosure has been made, unprompted by any fear of imminent discovery

- **Co-operation:** The maximum reduction is 40% and is given where information is provided promptly, questions are answered fully and correctly and if appropriate payments on account are made

- **Seriousness:** The maximum reduction is 40%, and again will depend on the overall seriousness of the matter – which could vary from incompetence to outright fraud.

In theory you could achieve a 100% reduction of the penalties but in practice that will rarely happen.

The new rules for penalties from the 2008/09 tax year do not override the pre-2008/09 rules, so if you find yourself with underpayments for a period spanning 2008 separate penalty calculations will have to be undertaken for each part of the period.

Now HMRC starts by specifying a maximum penalty, determined by what lead to the understatement. This could range from 'failing to take reasonable care' through to 'deliberately understating tax' or indeed 'taking steps to hide the understatement from HMRC'. It also allows a possible reduction according to whether the disclosure of the understatement was voluntary (i.e. you fessed up) or it was prompted by an actual or imminent HMRC intervention.

The table below shows how it all comes together:

	Starting-point penalty	Reduction in penalty potentially available	
		Enquiry initiated by HMRC	Voluntary unprompted disclosure
Negligence (failure to take "reasonable care")	30%	15%	30%
Deliberate understatement	70%	35%	50%
Concealed deliberate understatement	100%	50%	70%

The amount of the potential reduction achieved in a particular case will, as ever, depend on the extent to which you are considered to have assisted HMRC in getting everything back to normal.

Now up to 40% of the maximum potential reduction is available for promptly admitting, disclosing and explaining what's wrong; a further 30% for assisting in quantifying the liability and up to 30% for giving access to records and documents reasonably requested by HMRC to check the position. So again it is *possible* to achieve a 100% reduction.

As with every penalty which HMRC seeks to impose it is possible to appeal though, again, your accountant will be able to advise if you are wasting your valuable time.

Without scaring you completely (though if you want to evade you are probably not interested where HMRC suspects tax fraud or tax evasion) it can pursue matters either via a criminal prosecution or along civil lines. This is the nuclear option. To the extent that HMRC proceeds along a civil process, the investigation will be conducted in accordance with HMRC's Code of Practice 9 (COP9). Apologies for the jargon, but here it can't be explained any other way! Once HMRC issues COP9, they will, helpfully, offer an opportunity to disclose the nature of the tax fraud; this is known as the Contractual Disclosure Facility (CDF). Here the recalcitrant tax payer has three options:

- Own up

- Decide not to own up. (Denial is not the river in Africa and will prove financially painful)

- Ignore the CDF and again expect to ultimately get hit with financial penalties.

Needless to say if you know you've done wrong, the most sensible option is to own up, fully comply and get HMRC out of your life as quickly as possible unless, of course, you like paying expensive accountancy bills and clearly avoidable penalties.

Thanks

This has to start with thanks to Dad and Mum.

Though he's no longer here, for he died far too young at 65, Dad's values and beliefs live on through me and my younger brother Julian. Although it was not until Apollo 13 that we heard the phrase "failure is not an option", Dad practised it every day; he created not one, but two successful manufacturing companies, both started in different recessions. Was it tough for him? You bet, so please never use a recession as a reason as to why you can't make money in your business.

Cheers Dad – and it's a real shame that you are not around to see that, though we had a few scrapes along the way, your sons both did alright in the end.

Thanks, Mum, for always being there to pick us up when we fell over – and always having a "yes, you can" attitude.

You can choose your friends but not your family and in Julian, my younger brother, I have the best of both worlds. Sure, there's been some sibling rivalry but he's a true friend and trusted partner. We speak daily, whether to discuss last night's football or some business matter; I count myself lucky to have such a great relationship with him. He has completely smashed the 'Father, Son, Bankrupt' myth and runs a very sound ship that Dad would have been immensely proud of, as indeed am I. So, thanks Jules. 2012 proved a toughie for him as, within months of marrying the love of his life, Marcie was diagnosed with cancer which they both tackled full on and are now moving into very clear water and long may that continue.

Finally, and by no means last, all this would not be possible – or indeed worthwhile – without the love and support of Fenella. I have no doubt that sometimes it can't be easy being married to a Wallis, but your chirpiness and loving smile always shine through. You are the peas to my carrots, Jenny to Forest Gump, and I love you loads – which is why we celebrate our silver wedding anniversary in October.

Thank you for making me laugh at least once a day – along with keeping Blandford, Douglas and Fraser, not forgetting the irrepressible Sweep, in order.

Iain Wallis FCA July 2013